Another Way

Front cover image by Tobias Gale

Cover design by Christine Horner

Book design by David Miles

Edited by Sandy Draper

Proofread by Laura Pasquale

Decorative rays licensed from MiOli/Shutterstock.com.

ISBN 978-1-7349774-3-1 (paperback)

ISBN 978-1-7349774-2-4 (e-book)

Library of Congress Control Number: 2020920412

Published in Boulder, Colorado

www.tobiasgale.com

Another Way

A GUIDE TO UNDERSTANDING THE INNER CHILD AND A PATH TO RECLAIMING OUR DIVINITY

By Tobias Gale

Contents

Introduction....................1

A Loving Parent to Our Inner Child.................... 3

How to Use This Book.................... 4

Part I: Origin of the Inner Child.................... 7

Chapter 1: The Beginning....................9

The Origin of Separation.................... 11

The Repurposing of the Universe.................... 13

Chapter 2: The Inner Child 15

Core Child.................... 15

Wounded Child.................... 17

Wounded Self.................... 18

Chapter 3: Forgetting Who We Are 21

Chapter 4: Parent-Child Attachment....................25

Studies of Parent-Child Relationships.................... 26

Parenting Behavior and Attachment Styles 28

Chapter 5: The Manifestation of the Wounded Self....................33

Strategies to Cope with Separation.................... 35

A Range of Wounded Self Strategies... 39

Part II: Living from Our Wounded Self.................................. 41

Chapter 6: Strategies of the Wounded Self:
Dyadic Regulation..43

Repression of Our Authentic Self.. 44

Approval-Seeking... 46

Codependency 48

Chapter 7: Strategies of the Wounded Self:
Autoregulation..53

Attachment to Things.. 54

Doing and Self-Sufficiency... 55

Control of Our Environment... 57

Avoidance of Intimacy... 60

Chapter 8: Strategies of the Wounded Self:
Dissociation..63

Distraction 64

Addiction... 66

Suicide 68

Chapter 9: Cumulative Trauma and the Wounded Self................73

The Multiple Parts of Our Psyche... 75

Chapter 10: Coming Out of Denial..79

Part III: Becoming a Loving Parent to Our Inner Child........ 83

Chapter 11: Theology of the Inner Child,
Wounded Self, and Loving Parent..85

Becoming a Loving Parent.. 86

Guidance for the Way 89

Chapter 12: The Inherent Instinct of Our Loving Parent.............93
Processing Emotions Through Play and the Arts..................... 94

Chapter 13: Connection with God, the
Source of Unconditional Love...97
Creating a New Image of God.. 100

Chapter 14: Becoming a Loving Parent to
Our Wounded Child...103
Insecure-Disorganized/Disoriented Attachment.................. 105
Insecure-Avoidant Attachment.. 108
Insecure-Ambivalent Attachment... 113

Chapter 15: Secure Attachment with
Our Wounded Child...121
Feeling Our Wounded Child's Emotions................................ 122
Dialoguing with Our Wounded Child..................................... 126
Additional Practices.. 130
Maintaining Consistency and Intention................................ 132

Chapter 16: Healing the Trauma of Our Wounded Child.........139
Trauma Work in Practice... 141
Our Wounded Self's Resistance... 143
Surrendering to the Process.. 144

Chapter 17: Deepening Our Trust..147
Communicating with God... 150

Chapter 18: Becoming a Loving Parent to
Our Wounded Self..153
Changing Our Beliefs about Our Wounded Self.................... 154
Taking Responsibility for Our Wounded Self......................... 160
Forgiving Our Wounded Self.. 170

Chapter 19: Becoming a Loving Parent to Our Core Child.......175
Fostering a Relationship with Our Core Child 177
The Gifts of Relationship.. 182

Chapter 20: Supporting the Expression of
Our Authentic Self 185
Freeing Ourselves from the Norms.. 187

Chapter 21: Living from Integration...191

Chapter 22: Experiencing God's Love 195
Overcoming Separation 197

Part IV: Relationship with Others 203

Chapter 23: Loving Others..205
Putting Ourselves First... 207

Chapter 24: Forgiving Others 211
The Miracle of Forgiveness... 213

Chapter 25: Sharing Ourselves with Others 217
Healing in Relationships... 218

Chapter 26: Remembering Who We Are 221

Notes 223

Bibliography...231

Copyrights and Permissions 235

Introduction

The term "inner child" is fairly commonplace nowadays. We use it to refer to our innocent, playful desires, or hear it in the context of New Age pop culture. It is a term that we can feel in our bodies and hearts, but we may not consider its validity. Yet the Inner Child asks us to pay it more attention. It is everywhere (and that is no coincidence), more than in our casual references, but in fiction, poetry, religion, and psychology, more than in our lightness and joy, but in our suffering and pain. All sources of wisdom direct us back to the Inner Child. However, the journey is not in whatever we may know about the term but in our direct experience of it. Cultivating this experience is the purpose of *Another Way*.

I felt called to write this book. I had been in recovery from addiction for several years, and though I had experienced some relief from the insanity that had ruled my life, there was still deep pain within me, and anxieties left unexplained. When I was introduced to the concept of the Inner Child through a process called "Inner Bonding®,"[1] I began to connect the dots of my experience. It was as though a door had been opened, making way the possibility of transformation. Together with what I had learned in a 12-step program, my education in transpersonal counseling psychology, and the literary texts of *A Course in Miracles*[2] and *Conversations with God*,[3] a constellation of insight and understanding began to form. Each element became an integral part of the map that was creating itself as I learned how to become a Loving Parent to my Inner Child. I felt compelled to record each stage of my journey and soon realized that the material I was writing wasn't solely for myself but might benefit others too. The result is what became *Another Way*.

The title of this book refers to an event that was said to have inspired the writing of *A Course in Miracles*. The soon-to-be scribe, Helen Schucman, was having issues with a professional colleague, William Thetford, when he told her, unexpectedly, "he was tired of the angry and aggressive feelings [*their*] attitudes reflected, and concluded that 'there must be another way.'"[4]

While *Another Way's* primary focus is resolving conflict within ourselves rather than with others, the title is in honor of *A Course in Miracles*, which shaped much of the content of this book. It is also a statement offered in response to times when we feel stuck, lost, or hopeless on our journey: there is *another way* to live. *Another way* to relate to our experience. *Another way* to heal the trauma of our past and dysfunction of our present. *Another way* to open to the blessings that are inherently ours. I don't make a claim that what I'll be sharing with you is the *only* way… but *another way*. We are each guided toward a path that speaks uniquely to us, and while this book may be useful for some, it may not be for all.

A LOVING PARENT TO OUR INNER CHILD

Another Way is both theoretical and experiential, both metaphysical and embodied. It starts at the very beginning, before time, and extends into the not-so-distant future. However, most of the book is practical, focusing on the present, and how to become a Loving Parent to your Inner Child. Mary Ainsworth's research[5] was fundamental in helping me to understand the parent-child attachment relationship and to explain its impact on us in childhood. Insecure attachment relationships activate a part of the Inner Child called the "Wounded Self,"[6] which uses maladaptive strategies to meet our core needs. Those strategies that we adopt as children then become habitual patterns of behavior as adults in the form of codependency, addiction, the repression of our authentic self, and others. Although such strategies seek to experience God's love, they ultimately keep us separate from it because they disconnect us from our Inner Child—from the relationship where God's love is most intimately felt.

Reclaiming our divinity and experiencing freedom from suffering happens when we have a conscious relationship with our Inner Child; it mirrors the parent-child attachment, as our actions determine the nature of our Inner Child's attachment to us. If we are willing to change, then greater intimacy with our Inner Child can free us from old behaviors that keep us stuck and allow us to experience the unconditional love that is our birthright. And to help you navigate this process, I have shared examples that describe each stage of attachment with our Inner Child and specific tools to help facilitate change.

HOW TO USE THIS BOOK

The book is divided into four parts:

Part I, "Origin of the Inner Child," explores the relationship between God and God's Child and the sequence of events that led to the Child's embodiment within the physical universe. The manifestation of the Inner Child within human consciousness is then explained within the framework of the parent-child attachment relationship.

Part II, "Living from Our Wounded Self," describes the various Wounded Self strategies that we adopt in childhood in order to survive within our family and how these strategies become habitual patterns of behavior in adulthood.

In Part III, "Becoming a Loving Parent to Our Inner Child," we discover how our actions and attitudes toward our Inner Child reflect the ways in which we were parented, as well as the practical steps we can take to develop a secure attachment with them to heal past trauma and live with greater authenticity.

Finally, in Part IV, "Relationship with Others," we'll look at how becoming a Loving Parent to our Inner Child allows us to have more loving and honest relationships with others.

• • • • •

Another Way can be read as a companion to your own journey of becoming a Loving Parent to your Inner Child. The information contained within it is intended to serve as a guide. Reading the book only will do little; using it to facilitate healing can do much more.

While the majority of the material was gathered from my own experience, I use the collective "we" to make clear that *we* share the human condition, and *we* share the same possibility for recovery. (What are we recovering? The full and embodied expression of *who* we really are and *how* we are meant to experience life.) While we each have our own unique backgrounds and life history, we all have an Inner Child who needs us, regardless. It is my hope that by knowing we share some part of the same journey, the material in this book will feel more inclusive and accessible.

I use "God" to refer to the source of unconditional love and guidance needed on any journey of recovery. More than anything, it serves as a placeholder for a concept and reality and can be interchangeable with any other word of the same meaning. "God" is intentionally used without gender to broaden its image and diminish its patriarchal influence. At the same time, I am aware of the trauma and oppression that many have experienced in association with this word and speak directly to these issues in Chapter 13.

In closing, I want to express how grateful I am to have been given the opportunity to share this book with you. I do so because of how profoundly it has helped me. If there is any message that I hope you take away, it is that *you* are worthy and deserving of the most abundant love, and it is available for you to experience right *now*. The door is open.... Shall we walk through?

PART I

Origin of the Inner Child

We all carry within us an eternal child, a young being of innocence and wonder. And that symbolic child also carries us, who we have been, the record of our formative experiences, our pleasures and pains.... It is the soul of the person, created inside of us through the experiment of life.[7]

—JEREMIAH ABRAMS,
RECLAIMING THE INNER CHILD

CHAPTER 1

The Beginning

In the beginning, there was God. "God" is a way to describe what God is, and we could say that God is light, and God is love. The energy that is God is eternal and infinite. God was the beginning, and from God came more and more of what God is, for love begets love and light begets light. This act of expansion was creation, and this creation was an ever-extending of God's presence. As God gave all of what God was, there became a shared consciousness between God and the extension of God's self—which we can call God's "Child." Consciousness expanded, and this consciousness was One.

It is said that there was an instant in the infinity of God's consciousness when the Child, who was as much a part of God as God was to God's self, thought of being separate from God.[8] Although the thought was not reality, it created a new reality for God's Child, one in which the Child was no longer a part of God. Perhaps all the

Child wanted was to look upon themselves in God and know how they were loved. But doing so required a shift in consciousness—a stepping back from oneness with God—and in that shift, if even for the most minuscule lapse of time, the Child felt alone.

To make sense of feeling separate from God, the Child believed they had been abandoned. From thought comes experience, and so the Child's belief in their abandonment created their experience of abandonment. It was not light that was born from darkness, but rather darkness born from light. The pain of feeling abandoned by God was so great in contrast to what the Child had known that a dissociation took place within the Child's consciousness. The protective mechanism by which the Child dissociated was a part of the Child, which we can call the Child's "Wounded Self."[9] Because God created the Child in God's own image, the Child, too, had the power to create. Yet rather than create from love, the Child's Wounded Self created from fear. Scared to face the experience of being alone, the Child's Wounded Self created a new reality—the physical universe—to help them escape.

A way to conceptualize this event is by drawing a parallel to children, who in fear of an imagined reality, cover themselves with a blanket for protection. The blanket helps the child feel safe from what they believe might harm them. Similarly, the Child, in reaction to feeling abandoned by God, hid the entire body of their consciousness under the blanket of their imagination. The physical universe can, therefore, be understood as a false reality created by the Child's Wounded Self to protect them from feeling abandoned by God.

THE ORIGIN OF SEPARATION

The story of Adam and Eve describes the origin of God's Child and the creation of the physical universe. In the Torah, it is said that God placed Adam and Eve in the Garden of Eden, where there was also the Tree of Life and the Tree of Knowledge of Good and Evil. God tells them to never eat from the Tree of Knowledge of Good and Evil—that if done so, they "shall die."[10]

In the garden, the serpent tells Eve eating from The Tree of Knowledge of Good and Evil will not result in her and Adam's death, but in the opening of their eyes, and they "shall be as gods."[11] We know what happened next of course.... Both Adam and Eve eat from the tree, and the act is considered to be the "original sin" because it made them feel separate from God. Though the word "sin" has been given a particular connotation of having done something wrong or worthy of judgment, another meaning is to be "without" (*sine*, from Latin). This most accurately expresses Adam and Eve's experience, which is that of being *without* God. Like the Child, whose thought of separation creates the experience of separation, Adam and Eve's feeling of being without God was due to their belief that it was the consequence of their actions. "Death" referred not to that of the physical body, but to an experience of reality.

Adam and Eve's motivation to eat from the tree was to *experience* God, rather than be "as gods," just as the Child had intended when they stepped back from God's presence to know how they were loved. If the possibility for life and death was within the Garden of Eden, then what was the experience of the garden itself?

The Child, born from God's love, couldn't feel God's love, because they had nothing to compare it to. In an attempt to experience God's love, the Child divided their consciousness from God's to look upon and know what it was they were born from and into. Only as a result of feeling disconnected from God could the Child experience God; only in having first tasted death could Adam and Eve experience life.

Although the Child's intention was to experience God, the contrast was so startling that the Child forgot they had chosen to separate. It may be said that God's "warning" to never eat from the Tree of Knowledge of Good and Evil and "punishment" for having done so was merely a story the Child created to make sense of their experience. In the Child's forgetting, they believed they had done something wrong. And like Adam and Eve, who covered themselves with fig leaves and hid from God in fear of death, the Child covered themselves with the universe and hid in fear of a reality that never occurred.

"The Lord God called out to the man and said to him, 'Where are you?'"[12] searching for Adam and Eve like a parent looking for their lost child. Adam replied, "I heard you in the garden, and I was afraid because I was naked; so I hid."[13] Adam, like the Child, felt ashamed of his "nakedness"—of being who he was—because he no longer saw himself as innocent, but as unworthy of God's love. "Who told you that you were naked?"[14] said God, who just as well could have said, "Who told you that you did something wrong? That you were worthy of rejection? That I abandoned you?" But it was too late. The Child, symbolized by Adam and Eve, believed in the wound and in their unworthiness and couldn't receive the truth from God from underneath the blanket they'd created.

THE REPURPOSING OF THE UNIVERSE

The Child embodied within the physical universe, born into a new consciousness in which the wound of their abandonment and belief in their unworthiness was buried. The strategy of the Child's Wounded Self was not only to keep them safe in a dream, removed from the nightmare that was the "truth" but to help the Child reclaim their worth through the world's approval and rewrite the story that the Child of God is unlovable. The problem, however, was that creating the universe as a way to distract the Child from their trauma separated them from the knowledge and experience of God's love.

When the Wounded Self created the universe, the consciousness of all creatures was made in the image of fear. This primitive reptile brain was oriented toward fight or flight instead of giving and receiving love. God witnessed what occurred and, in God's love for God's Child, saw the universe as an opportunity to help them experience what they sought from the beginning. God knew that in relationship—in the coming together as one—the Child could realize the dream they had created and awaken to the truth of their reality. And so God guided the evolution of the creatures, developing the brain and nervous system until at last the human being was formed. In human consciousness, God saw it possible for the Child to know and experience God's love and "found it very good."[15] God said to them, "Be fertile and increase, fill the earth and master it."[16] Such was the repurposing of the universe.

CHAPTER 2

The Inner Child

The entire universe, every living being, every aspect of nature is a part of God and contains the Child of God within it. The Child that is an extension of God in the absolute reality also exists within us as the core of our own personal soul. This Child is the archetype that drives the human impulse toward the complete recollection of our true self and the experience of God. It is this core aspect of our soul that descended into the physical reality to experience God's love.

CORE CHILD

When we are born, we are the Child manifested in physical form—open, vulnerable, ready to receive, and experience unconditional love. This is why we embodied, so we could know God's love experientially.[17] The Core Child, referred to by Margaret Paul as the "core Self," is the "unwounded aspect of the soul."[18] The birth of this Child in us creates a state of complete openness and sensitivity to our environment, as the Child is born naked and with nothing to fear—nothing to protect against.

Our Core Child "contains our unique gifts and talents, our natural wisdom and intuition, our curiosity and sense of wonder, our playfulness and spontaneity, and our ability to love."[19] We can see this Child in an infant, who looks upon the world with wonder and looks into the eyes of another through God's eyes. We can also find this Child in nature, in the sky, in the clouds, in the mountains and rivers, in the coming together of a community or family in the name of love. We all have this inherent wakefulness within us, but it must be nurtured. To make fertile ground for the seed within us to grow, our parents and society must create an environment that promotes this growth.

When we are born, we are God's Child brought forth into the physical reality, but we are entirely reliant upon the world to teach us this truth. To know the truth about ourselves, we must be raised by parents or caregivers who can show us unconditional love, who can teach us that we are Children of God.

As children, we look to our parents to embody God's love through meeting our emotional, psychological, and physical needs. As long as our needs are met, and we experience safety and security, our Core Child is free to express themselves. We may remain in this unified state of consciousness with our parents for some time, as in the following illustration:

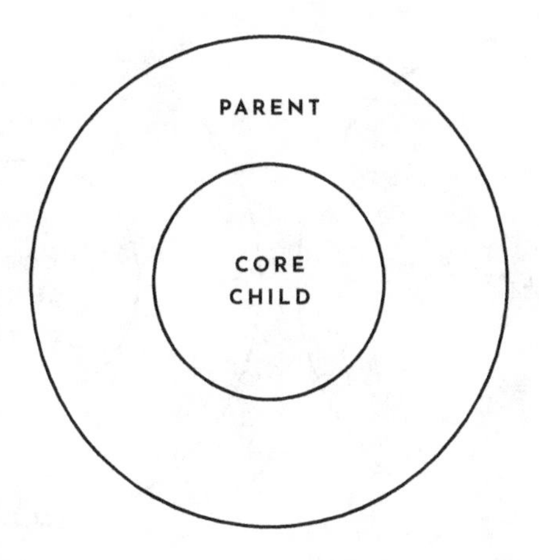

The large circle represents the parent, and the smaller circle represents the Core Child. This psychic relationship is experienced within the consciousness of the human child.

WOUNDED CHILD

The process by which the physical universe was created—where God's Child thought of being separate from God, and the Child's Wounded Self manifested to "protect" the Child—is reenacted in the parent-child relationship. When the child's primary needs are not met, when unconditional love is not given, the child experiences wounding or trauma. As a result, they feel separate from their parent—from the love that was their sense of safety and security, as the illustration below shows:

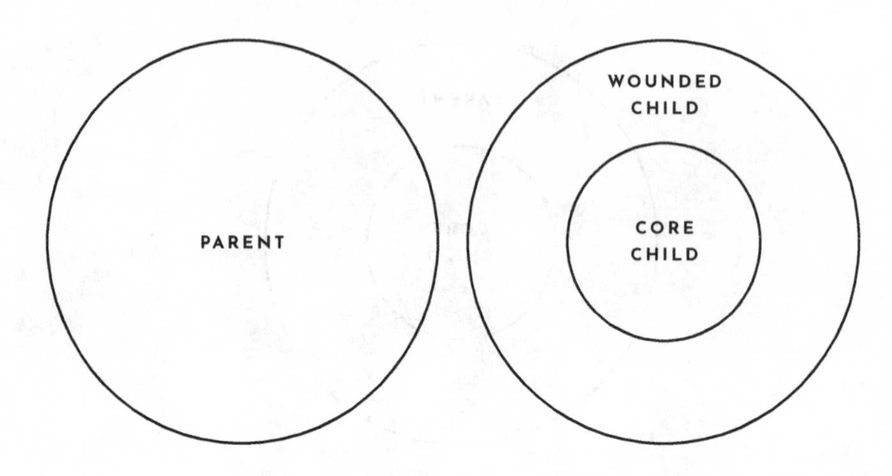

As a result of trauma, the child no longer experiences themselves as safe and secure within their parent's care, but rather outside of the container that held them. This event creates a layer of wounding around the Core Child, and it changes their perception and experience of reality. They feel abandoned by their parent, and like the Child who felt abandoned by God, develop the unconscious belief of being unworthy of their parents' love and somehow deserving of this rejection. The human child, who was once the manifestation of their unwounded soul, becomes a Wounded Child.[20]

WOUNDED SELF

Due to their inability to tolerate the emotional and psychological distress caused by such trauma, the child dissociates. The defense mechanism employed by the child's psyche to survive feeling rejected and abandoned is the same mechanism used by God's Child. The Wounded Self operates in the personal unconscious[21] of the human child to protect them from further harm, as the illustration below shows:

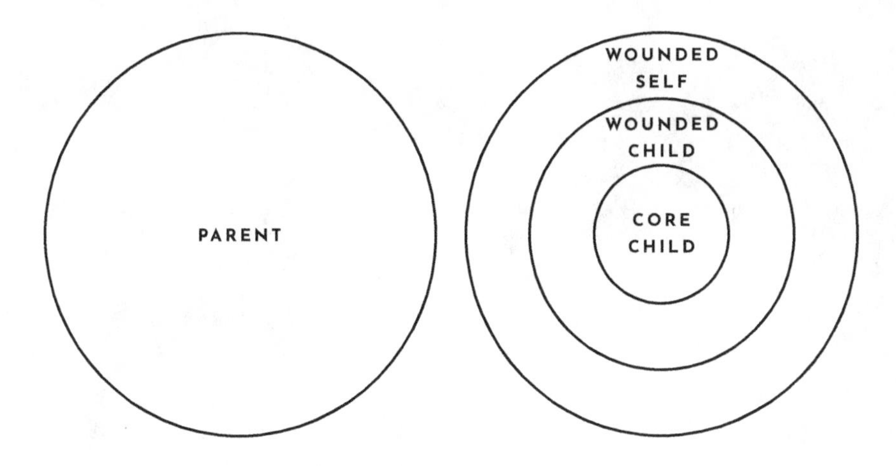

The child's psyche develops two substructures that surround the Core Child. The Wounded Child embodies the spiritual, emotional, and psychological impact of the trauma, and the Wounded Self is the psyche's defense mechanism used in reaction to it. We can, therefore, conceptualize the Inner Child as being made up of three substructures. Depicted as concentric circles, the Wounded Self occupies the exterior, the Wounded Child the middle, and the Core Child the interior. Further on, we will discuss the nature of each substructure as expressed within the human experience.

CHAPTER 3

Forgetting Who We Are

Every family has a culture of dysfunction that is passed down from generation to generation. Our parents learned it from their families, and their parents learned it from theirs. A particular family's culture is influenced by society's culture. Dysfunction is a way to describe a blockage of our authentic expression and the honoring of our core needs—namely, unconditional love. Dysfunction happens when there are oppressive messages that say it's not okay to be who we are, that we must conform and inhibit the expressions of what makes us *us,* in order to be loved; that there are more important things to direct our attention to than loving ourselves and our children. If we knew how to love ourselves in all of our emotions, in all of our experiences in response to life, then we would be able to meet these needs of our children.

The core wound of the Child was in feeling separate from the love and care of God. Because in each of us exists the Child of God, so in each of us exists the Child's core wound of feeling unlovable and the core fear of not being cared for. The creation of the universe was an attempt by the Wounded Self to help the Child forget this wound, but the result was that we forgot the truth that we are wholly lovable and in the care of God. When we know our own wholeness, we are not compelled to grasp for love from a place of lack. We don't give the world the power to tell us about our lovability. We are a fountain that is continuously filled by God's love and cannot help but let this love flow unto our children. In the receiving of our unconditional love, our children come to know that they too are wholly loveable, and in this, the truth of who we are is passed down generation to generation.

When we forget that we are wholly lovable and in the care of God, the consciousness of the Wounded Self enters our mind. As a result, the Child of God hears the voice of fear and becomes afraid. Where once the Child was free in the giving and receiving of love, now they believe they are alone, left to fend for themselves to survive. We hear our Inner Child's fear, but rather than comfort them as a parent would, reassuring them that the nightmare of their sleep was just a dream, we believe the Child, and the false belief becomes a new reality. When we think that we are separate from the unconditional love and care of God, we cease to be a fountain and become a dry well. Our priority becomes the filling of this well, and our attention moves outward to fill it.

The knowledge of being in God's unconditional love and care has now faded from the culture of a family and of society. No longer do we give and receive love, but fear—the belief that we must fight for security, compete for our basic needs to be met, and perform and accomplish for the approval of others. When we forget that we are loved and cared for by God, we live our lives in fear; it enters our culture, our family system and becomes the primary influence of the collective consciousness. As our consciousness becomes more and more influenced by fear, we move away from our center; we lose our ground. The Child in us becomes afraid because we, the parents of this Child, have fallen into the dream of scarcity and lack. We look to the world to obtain what we believe we don't already have and forget our God-given purpose of loving our Inner Child.

This is what has happened for much of humanity, and this is the state of our collective consciousness. Our families and society no longer teach us how to love ourselves, how to feel pain, and how to heal trauma—all this has been forgotten in the dream spun by the Wounded Self. Interconnectedness dissolves as fear occupies more space within our minds. We cease being brothers and sisters and become enemies. In our inability to love ourselves unconditionally, we are unable to love others unconditionally. Violence occurs—hatred, oppression, abuse, and genocide—all in the confused expression of our own internal pain, all in a vain attempt to create a greater sense of security for the Child lost within us.

CHAPTER 4

Parent-Child Attachment

Raising a child is about protecting and nourishing their innocence, their freedom, and the holiness given to them by God. This is our most vital task, because if we are given the freedom to be who we really are, then God's love can most easily manifest in the world.

Intergenerational trauma occurs when we don't recognize the truth of who we are nor love ourselves in ways that enable us to raise Children of God. We all have had parents who have had parents that could not accomplish this tremendously difficult task—difficult because we are conditioned to *not* live in this way nor to think of ourselves as wholly worthy of our own love, and of God's love. If we don't value ourselves in this way, we cannot value our children in this way, and they grow up not knowing who they really are.

STUDIES OF PARENT-CHILD RELATIONSHIPS

A way to better understand the effects of parenting on us is by looking at parent-child attachment relationships. As I mentioned in the Introduction, one of the most influential studies was by Mary Ainsworth, who published the first results of her research in 1969. Ainsworth and her colleagues observed 106 infants from white, middle-class families in the Baltimore area. Twenty-six of these infants were a part of a longitudinal study, and they were observed at home with their mothers during four-hour sessions, approximately every three weeks, from three to fifty-four weeks of age. All the infants were then observed in the Strange Situation Procedure.[22] This laboratory study sought to simulate the day-to-day experience of the parent-child relationship.

The Strange Situation Procedure consisted of eight, three-minute episodes (aside from the first, which was one minute). These episodes were designed to encourage the infant's exploratory behavior (i.e., play), then, through a series of mildly stressful events, to observe if and how the child sought out the parent for emotional comfort.[23] A brief explanation of the experiment is as follows.

Episode 1: The mother carries her infant into a room filled with toys. Episode 2: The mother places her infant on the floor, encourages them to play with the toys, and then sits in a chair close by. Episode 3: A "stranger" (someone who was a part of the experiment but unfamiliar to the infant) enters the room, sits in another chair, and begins a conversation with the mother. Episode 4: The mother exits the room, leaving her infant alone with the stranger. Episode 5: The mother returns, the stranger exits the room, and the mother is alone with her infant. Episode 6: The mother exits the room for a second time, leaving her infant completely alone. Episode 7: The stranger enters the room and is alone with the infant. Episode 8: The mother returns, the stranger exits the room, and the mother is alone with her infant for a final reunion.

It was believed that when the parent-child relationship was intact, the infant used their parent as a secure base from which to actively explore their environment. But when the parent-child relationship felt threatened, the infant would seek close proximity and contact with the parent.[24] The results of the study revealed that the infants displayed different types of attachment behavior in response to the separation and reunion episodes. Because the Strange Situation Procedure was standardized, so that each set of eight episodes was identical for every infant, disparities in behavior suggested disparities in the parent-child attachment relationship.[25]

The Strange Situation Procedure identified three types of attachment styles:

- secure
- insecure-ambivalent
- insecure-avoidant

Each attachment style was characterized by specific attachment behaviors throughout the experiment.

Infants classified as "secure" used their parent as a base from which to explore their environment and engage in play. If they were distressed by their parent's absence during separation episodes, they were quickly comforted and soothed by their parent's return, thus allowing them to return to play and exploration.[26]

Infants classified as "insecure-ambivalent" were the most anxious among the group. They were often distressed before separation with their parent, extremely distressed during separation, and showed strong proximity/contact seeking behavior upon reunion, which was often coupled with resistance and anger.[27] Due to their distress, these infants exhibited the least amount of exploratory and play behavior.

Infants classified as "insecure-avoidant" spent more time exploring their environment than interacting with their parent. Such "play" behavior, however, was found to be without vitality. Rather than for enjoyment, the play was believed to be a way of coping with their distress.[28] Their high level of activation, though not vocalized (e.g., crying), was evidenced by strong search behavior during separation episodes. Yet unlike the infants with a secure attachment, those with an insecure-avoidant attachment style actively avoided or ignored their parent upon reunion.

PARENTING BEHAVIOR AND ATTACHMENT STYLES

Following the findings of the Strange Situation Procedure, Ainsworth[29] used the data from the home observations to examine how parenting behavior correlated to infant attachment styles. At home, it was found that mothers of securely attached infants were sensitive and responsive to their infant's signals and communications, prompt in responding to their infant crying, and affectionate during close physical contact.

At home, the behavior of infants with a secure attachment style was similar to that shown in the Strange Situation Procedure; they exhibited positive behavior toward their mothers and spent a lot of time in exploration and play. During face-to-face encounters, they displayed positive responses by smiling, vocalizing, and bouncing. They enjoyed close physical contact and were quickly soothed by it when distressed. Additionally, infants with a secure attachment were unlikely to cry when their mothers left the room, which was reflective of the infant's confidence in their mother's accessibility.[30]

During the home observations, mothers of infants with an insecure-ambivalent attachment style were found to be insensitive and less responsive to infant signals, crying, and communication. Though not averse to close physical contact, they held their infants with little affection or skill and often did so while engaged in routine activities. They were less accepting and more rejecting of their infant's behavior than mothers of securely attached infants.

The home behavior of infants with an insecure-ambivalent attachment style was similar to that in the Strange Situation Procedure. They were anxious with their mother, slower to be soothed than securely attached infants, and cried frequently. Though not averse to close physical contact, they reacted angrily toward their mother if not picked up when they wanted to be held or when put down too soon. They lacked confidence in their mother's responsiveness and accessibility, which was thought to be a significant source of distress.

During the home observations, mothers of infants with an insecure-avoidant attachment style were found to be insensitive, ignoring, and rejecting of their infant's signals and communications. They took longer to respond to crying than mothers of securely attached infants. They were often angry with their infants, which was expressed through rough handling, aversion to close physical contact, using physical force to back up verbal commands, and being abrupt and interfering when picking them up. Additionally, they were frequently irritated when the needs of their infant interfered with their personal life and allowed feelings of resentment to overpower more positive feelings for their infant.[31]

At home, infants with an insecure-avoidant attachment style cried frequently and were distressed when their mother left the room. They were also conflicted about their desire for close physical contact. Though they would at times seek proximity and closeness, they would just as often avoid it, because contact with their mother, despite being an intrinsic need, was an unpleasant experience.

• • • • •

Mary Ainsworth's research, while helpful in identifying parent-child dynamics that contribute to infant attachment styles, is limited in its generalizability due to its small sample size and homogenous demographic. As parent-child attachment is a human phenomenon, it is essential to assess whether Ainsworth's Strange Situation Procedure and the infant attachment styles associated with it apply to children from other cultures and backgrounds. IJzendoorn and Kroonenberg[32] conducted a meta-analysis of studies from eight different countries (Germany, UK, the Netherlands, Sweden, Israel, Japan, China, and the United States) that used Ainsworth's Strange Situation Procedure to identify infant attachment styles. In total, there were 32 samples and 1,990 Strange Situation classifications.

Among all the samples, secure attachment style was the most common among infants. However, there were notable cross-cultural differences: insecure-avoidant attachment style was the second most common among infants from Germany, U.K., the Netherlands, and Sweden, and insecure-ambivalent attachment style was the second most common among infants from Israel and Japan. In a sample of infants from China, there was an equal representation of insecure-avoidant and insecure-ambivalent attachment styles following secure attachment. In the U.S., attachment styles between samples were the most variant. While secure attachment style was predominant, the groups differed in having insecure-avoidant or insecure-ambivalent attachment style as the second most common.

An important finding was that sample differences within a country were much greater than those between countries. For instance, a particular U.S. sample more closely resembled one from Israel than any other U.S. sample, and a sample from Tokyo was more similar to two U.S. samples than it was to a sample from

Sapporo, another Japanese city. The variation among U.S. samples was partly attributed to their demographic diversity. Easterbrooks and Lamb's[33] sample, which was made up of "middle-class, mostly professional families,"[34] had fewer insecurely attached infants. In contrast, three other U.S. samples[35], which all involved families of "low socioeconomic status and included, respectively, black infants from a low-income population, economically disadvantaged and martially unstable families, and a number of maltreated infants"[36] had a much higher number of insecurely attached infants.

The results of IJzendoorn and Kroonenberg's research indicate that the Strange Situation Procedure is a valid measurement for identifying attachment styles of infants from diverse cultural and socioeconomic backgrounds. Moreover, attachment styles, in general, can be classified as secure, insecure-avoidant, and insecure-ambivalent.[37] Some critical factors shown to influence attachment styles are the family's sub-culture (more than their country of origin) and environmental stress associated with low-socioeconomic status. When parents interact with their children, they are not only guided by social norms and customs, but by their emotional, psychological, and spiritual health, which is a byproduct of their social location.

CHAPTER 5

The Manifestation of the Wounded Self

Mary Ainsworth's research not only demonstrates the impact that parental behavior has on our psychological and emotional wellbeing but offers clues as to how the Inner Child is affected by the parent-child relationship. In a secure attachment relationship, the child feels safe, trusts in their parent's ability to meet their needs, and can easily engage in exploration and play. In other words, the child experiences their parent's unconditional love and, as a result, can live and express themselves from their Core Child. Referring back to the diagram of the Core Child, a secure attachment relationship would look like this:

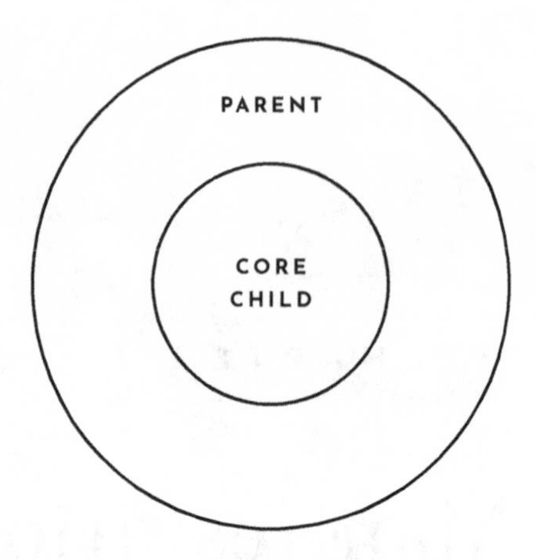

When held within the container of our parent's love, our consciousness is the manifestation of our Core Child. However, these dynamics change in an insecure attachment relationship. Ainsworth[38] explains that a child's attachment behavior and exploratory behavior are incompatible. When a parent is insensitive or unresponsive to their child's signals and communications, rejects their behavior, or is unaffectionate or averse to close physical contact, the child experiences trauma, which is most clearly expressed by their difficulty or inability to engage in play. Whether it happens abruptly (i.e., acute) or over time (i.e., cumulative), trauma forces the Inner Child out of their psychological womb. As a result, the child's consciousness, which is reflected in their behavior, becomes that of the Wounded Child. The diagram to depict this change would look like this:

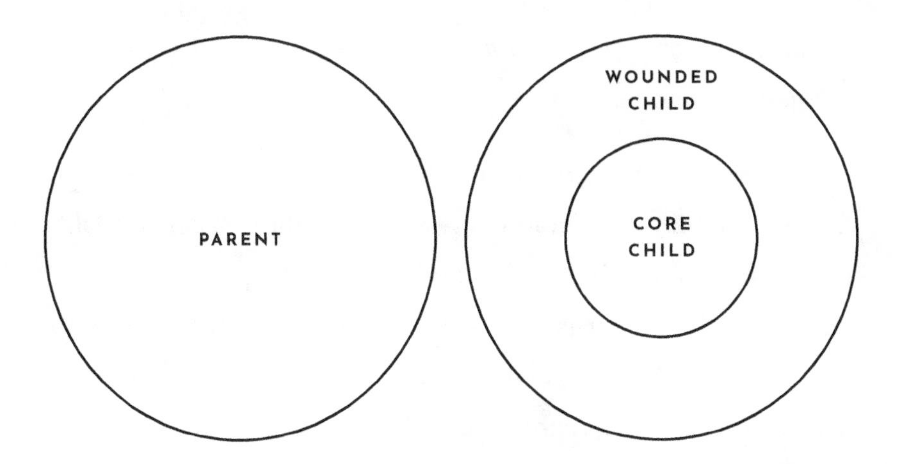

The Inner Child is now separate from the psychic container of the parent's love, and the Core Child is covered over by the Wounded Child. However, this state of consciousness doesn't last long. Feeling alone and unprotected, the child learns to adopt strategies to survive within the family system.

STRATEGIES TO COPE WITH SEPARATION

Mary Ainsworth's research showed that infants, depending upon their style of attachment, used varying strategies—or ways of organizing their behavior—to manage their distress. The securely attached infant has a clear and coherent strategy. When the attachment feels threatened in some way, the child signals to their parent to increase proximity and closeness. As Main and Solomon noted:

> *For these infants, there is a relatively smooth alternation between attachment behavior and exploratory behavior with one or the other receiving emphasis, dependent upon the*

> *accessibility of the attachment figure and the initial 'strangeness' of the situation.*[39]

When a parent adequately meets their infant's needs, it encourages the infant's ability to tolerate distress.[40] When the parent is available, the infant looks to them to be soothed (i.e., "dyadic regulation"[41]), and when the parent is unavailable, they self-soothe (i.e., "autoregulation"[42]). While this form of self-soothing is rudimentary, the infant's trust in their parent's care for them (and responsiveness should they need them) offers the infant a buffer against the anxiety of being left alone.

When the infant is without a parent whom they can depend upon or feel safe with, they are left without the means to effectively regulate their distress.[43] In such cases, the infant's psyche responds by manifesting a Wounded Self, an aspect of the Inner Child that organizes the infant's behavior to engender a sense of security and love. In an insecure attachment relationship, the Wounded Self manifests as a layer surrounding the Wounded Child. A diagram to depict this adaptation would like this:

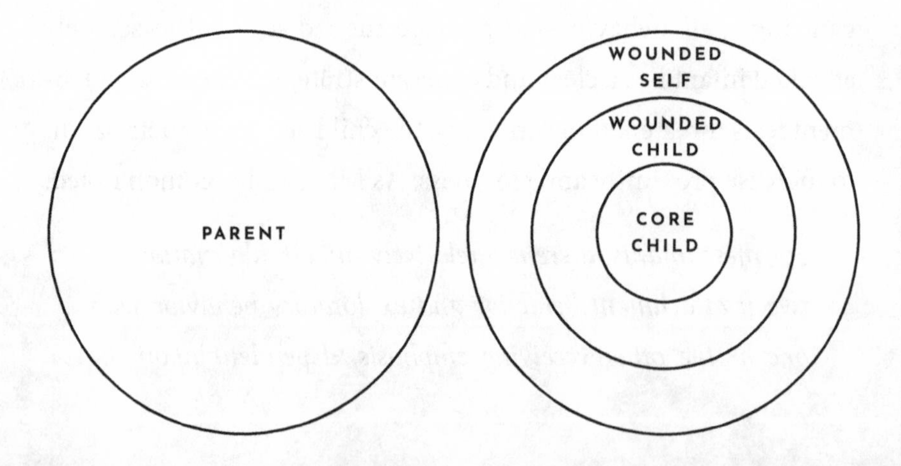

In contrast to the strategies of a secure attachment style, the Wounded Self strategies of an insecurely attached infant arise from a dysregulated state. Schore explains:

> *The human infant's psychobiological response to trauma is comprised of two separate response patterns—hyperarousal and dissociation. In the initial stage of threat, a startle or alarm reaction is initiated, in which the sympathetic component of the autonomic nervous system (ANS) is suddenly and significantly activated.*[44]

Infants with an insecure-ambivalent attachment style and insecure-avoidant attachment style both exhibit this hyperarousal response to trauma. However, the strategies used by each infant to cope with their distress differ.

As opposed to the securely attached infant who has internalized their parent's accessibility and responsiveness, infants with an insecure-ambivalent attachment style have an "internal representation"[45] of a parent who is insensitive and unreliable. Without developing a capacity to self-soothe, they depend on their parent for emotional regulation. The maintenance of this attachment relationship becomes all-important for the infant, which is exhibited by their anxious preoccupation with their parent's comings and goings and their clingy behavior during close physical contact.[46] It may be that by monitoring the parent's behavior, these infants could better anticipate being left alone, and by clinging, could prevent it from happening. It is the Wounded Self, born from the fear of scarcity and lack, which motivates the infant's strategies.

While they do little to regulate the infant's distress, they are the only options available.

Infants with an insecure-avoidant attachment style use a maladaptive form of autoregulation to cope with their distress. Due to their parent's aversion to close physical contact, irritation with their behavior, and rejection, these infants feel safer avoiding their parents instead of seeking closeness with them. Without a parent to turn to for comfort and without the capacity to self-soothe, these infants look to things in their environment to cope. As shown in the Strange Situation Procedure, when distressed by both the novelty of the circumstance and their parent's behavior, these infants spent the majority of their time playing with toys. This strategy, however, did little to relieve their anxiety.[47] If anything, it served as a temporary distraction.

When an infant's level of distress exceeds their tolerance, and they are without an external source for regulation, they move beyond a state of hyperarousal to one of dissociation. As Schore notes:

> [This] *later-forming reaction to infant trauma... in which the child disengages from stimuli in the external world and attends to an 'internal' world... involves numbing, avoidance, compliance, and restricted affect.*[48]

Mary Main, a student of Mary Ainsworth, observed 55 infants in the Strange Situation Procedure who displayed these "inexplicable, 'odd,' or conflicted patterns of behavior."[49] Unclassified under Ainsworth's three attachment styles, they were given a new status of Insecure-Disorganized/Disoriented.

It was found that infants with an insecure-disorganized/disoriented attachment style were frequently from high-risk conditions and experienced maltreatment, abuse, and neglect.[50] In the Strange Situation, they showed no obvious or coherent attachment strategy to alleviate their distress. Due to having a parent that was both "the source of and the solution to its alarm,"[51] such infants exhibited more of a freeze response than fight or flight. Schore explains:

> *The purpose of this primitive defensive reaction is to protect the developing organism against the overwhelming psychobiological pain of the attachment disruptions induced by early relational trauma.*[52]

Though effective in helping the infant survive their experience, such dissociative strategies become habitual reactions to distress.

A RANGE OF WOUNDED SELF STRATEGIES

The manifestation of the Wounded Self is an involuntary reaction to threat—the infant's consciousness in a dysregulated state. Just as the primary responsibility of a parent is the regulation of their infant's distress,[53] so it becomes the responsibility of the Wounded Self. When the parent is inattentive and lacking in care, the Wounded Self manifests to help the infant cope. They either grasp for what is available from their parents, look to the environment to displace their anxiety, or dissociate completely. Although the attachment styles have been categorized by specific strategies, such behaviors are more on a continuum than in discrete boxes. For instance, while one infant may use strategies that are characteristic of an insecure-ambivalent attachment style, they may also, at times, use those of an insecure-avoidant attachment style. Even infants that are securely attached may occasionally use Wounded Self strategies to alleviate their distress. Each particular strategy is adopted and used in response to specific circumstances. Depending upon the severity of their distress and the safety of their environment, infants may resort to an entire spectrum of strategies to cope.

If the infant's Wounded Self strategies are on a continuum, it is reasonable to expect that dissociation is not only used by infants with an insecure-disorganized/disoriented attachment style but also by those with other attachment styles. The determining factor is how overwhelmed the infant feels and how well they can cope with their distress. When the infant is in a chronic state of anxiety due to an internalized absence of safety, the Wounded Self engages in dissociation to reduce the infant's sensitivity to their trauma.

Another reason why an infant might display a range of Wounded Self strategies may be due to having a different attachment relationship to each parent. While one parent may be sensitive, responsive, and affectionate, the other may be rejecting, unavailable, and averse to close physical contact. The infant's attachment behaviors with each parent will, therefore, differ. However, the range of strategies remains within the Wounded Self's memory and finds new and more complex expressions as the child grows up.

PART II

Living from Our Wounded Self

He whom I enclose with my name is weeping in this dungeon. I am ever busy building this wall all around; and as this wall goes up into the sky day by day I lose sight of my true being in its dark shadow.[54]

—RABINDRANATH TAGORE, *GITANJALI*

CHAPTER 6

Strategies of the Wounded Self: Dyadic Regulation

As children, we are highly sensitive. We are not born open, without defenses, in order to be wounded. We are born in the openness of our souls to receive the unconditional love from our parents that God wills for us to experience. Yet, as a result of trauma, we no longer experience ourselves in the container that was our parents' love. Outside of this container, all circumstances become threatening. In the "protection" of our Wounded Self, we seek the love that we had become estranged from or avoid the pain of feeling rejected and abandoned.

Growing up, we quickly learned whether or not it was safe to be ourselves, whether it was okay to be sad or angry, to dance or sing, to laugh or play, to say and express how we were feeling. We learned whether or not we would receive loving support when we needed it. If we experienced any form of rejection in the expression of our authentic self, then we repressed our authenticity to avoid the pain of rejection. This may have been one of the first Wounded Self strategies of dyadic regulation that we used.

REPRESSION OF OUR AUTHENTIC SELF

It was our parents' actions that conveyed whether we were lovable or not. If our parents didn't comfort us when we were afraid, hold us when we needed affection, or emotional support, we told ourselves that it was because *we* were unlovable. If we were to believe the problem resided in our parents' ability to meet our needs, then that would set us up with the terrifying reality that such needs would never be fulfilled. If we believed that *we* were the cause of our parent's rejection and abandonment, then we could control how and when we received our parents' love.

We learned from our parents which emotions were okay to express and which ones weren't. The "negative" emotions produced negative results because they discomforted our parents, and the "positive" emotions produced positive ones. When our parents were unable to be present, or tolerate, their own feelings of sadness, depression, anxiety, anger, or joy, then they couldn't support our expression of these emotions. As a result, we learned that expressing these emotions led to our experience of rejection.

Western culture is an expression of the strategies we learn to avoid the pain of rejection. Songs such as the classic, "Santa Claus is Coming to Town," known to most children whether or not they celebrate Christmas, exclaims how we "better not cry," and we "better not pout," for if we do we are "naughty" or "bad." By being "good for goodness sake," we are better able to receive the presents of our parents' conditional love. This song speaks to how sadness and anger are socially unacceptable. But the song, like our culture, doesn't view the problem as residing in our parents' inability to be present and compassionate toward us in our emotions, but that we are "bad" for merely having them. This is the message that so often runs through families and is passed down to the next generation.

If, in our sadness, we were ignored, and in our anger, we were punished, if in our anxiety, we were invalidated, and in our playfulness, we were ridiculed, then we repressed these emotions to remain lovable. We learned to be dishonest about how we were feeling to avoid rejection. Additionally, we learned that our parents weren't safe to go to for emotional support. We became isolated in our suffering without the help we needed to process and express our feelings.

Growing up with the message that it's not okay to live from our authentic selves and to express our emotions causes us to reject our Inner Child, because our Inner Child is most visibly expressed in just that way. If we were never taught how to feel our emotions nor that having them could bring positive results, how are we to have a healthy relationship with them today? We needed our parents to show us that it was acceptable and normal to have emotions. We needed our parents to help us feel these emotions, because we lacked the physiological capacity to hold and process them on our own.

When we were rejected for expressing ourselves, we were not only given the message that our emotions were bad, but that *we* were bad—that we were unworthy of unconditional love. We learned that if others didn't love us in our emotions, then we shouldn't love ourselves in our emotions—that they were something to be ashamed and embarrassed about, something to hide. The unfortunate byproduct of emotional repression also suppressed our Core Child—the aspect of the Inner Child that lies beneath the wounding of our life experiences. And so the strategy of repressing our emotions came at a cost. We could play, but no longer in an endless field. We could sing and dance, but our melody and movement were stuck and limited by our pain. Without the freedom to express our authentic selves, we could no longer be children.

APPROVAL-SEEKING

Approval-seeking is another Wounded Self strategy whereby we seek out someone else's approval to regulate our Inner Child's fear of being unlovable. Initially, the love we sought was from our parents. We became willing to play the game of perfectionism and people-pleasing to get our need for love met. We learned what it meant to be a "good" boy or girl and what we had to do to receive such praise. Perhaps being a diligent student, using our intellect and intelligence and earning high grades, was a way in which we could receive our parents' approval. We may have had a natural inclination toward the arts, music, or sports, and excelled in these areas for recognition. Our Inner Child may very well have enjoyed such activities as a way of emotional expression, to connect with others, and experience our own creative and physical potential. But our Wounded Self was also aware that these activities could offer us glimpses of our parents' love, and so part of our motivation for being an accomplished student, artist, or athlete may have been for these rewards.

As we grew up, we carried the strategies of repression and approval-seeking into our other social environments. If our parents couldn't give us the message that we were worthy of love, then maybe our friends could, or our teachers. In school, we also learned which norms of expression were acceptable and which weren't. We had a need to belong, and so we willingly compromised our authentic selves to fit into the crowd. Perhaps we dressed as others dressed, liked what others liked, laughed at what others laughed at, or even started to smoke or drink alcohol. Belonging was a way in which we could feel loved, and our Wounded Self was willing to let go of our authentic selves to meet this need.

No matter how "good" we were, the moment we fell short of our parents' expectations or of society's norms, we experienced some form of rejection. Perfectionism is a result of this universal core wound. When we are not given unconditional love, we end up believing that we need to be "perfect" to be loved. So much of the world thrives on perfectionism. When we can show others how perfect we are in what we *do,* then we feel that we have worth and value.

This is the story that our Wounded Self plays over and over again. And it is a sad song, because it screams in its statement that it is the truth; and yet as long as we believe it, we neglect to realize that it is, in fact, a dream. Society, driven by the collective Wounded Self, is entirely unconscious of the truth; that is inherent within us—which is that our worth, value and lovability is given to us by God regardless of what we do, or don't do, or what we accomplish or achieve, and is forever unchangeable.

CODEPENDENCY

Another Wounded Self strategy is codependency, which is the transference of our attachment relationship with our parents onto our relationships with others, particularly significant others. If, as children, we had an insecure-ambivalent attachment style and our primary source for regulation was our parents, we grow into adulthood and use the same strategy with our partners. Without much capacity for self-regulation and with a preference for dyadic regulation, we rely on this strategy for managing or soothing distress. The strategy becomes habitual and depending upon another person to feel safe and loved becomes a trait.

It may have been in adolescence when our codependency first became pronounced. We sought in a boyfriend or girlfriend the feeling of unconditional love. We lived for the ecstasy of romance. Perhaps we dreamed of our romantic interest from morning till night, creating stories of a perfect life together, and how all of our needs were going to be met now that we had found "the one." And when the relationship failed to meet our expectations, we were cast into weeks, months, or years of depression and despair—at least until we found another person who could fill this role.

The influence of our culture upon the strategy of codependency is extraordinary. The songs played on the radio are mostly about needing another person's love to be okay. Such is also the case in movies, TV, and social media. These messages perpetuate the belief that only through others can we feel whole and only in a romantic relationship is life worth living. When we conform to these beliefs, we are bound to feel as though we are missing something important, something intrinsic to our sense of self. We become willing to do a great deal and go to any lengths to find and keep that special someone.

A consequence of codependency is that we lose ourselves in relationships with others. We let go of our authentic self and our needs to maintain another person's love. We abandon our Inner Child for the sake of the relationship. Just as we compromised ourselves to be loved by our parents, so we compromise ourselves to be loved by our partner. Of course, another consequence of codependency is feeling angry when our partner cannot satisfy our unmet childhood needs. As *A Course in Miracles* says, "When you are angry, is it not because someone has failed to fill the function you allotted him?"[55] It's always easier to be resentful toward others for what they are unable to give us than look at how we still hold unrealistic expectations.

In our Wounded Self, we look to others to tell us of our worth, value, and lovability. Every relationship becomes a reconstruction of our relationship with our parents. We hope to experience the truth of who we are and that someone might love us in a way that our parents never could. Yet when we give our power to others to tell us who we are, we believe that how we are treated is indicative of what we deserve.

• • • • •

The Wounded Self strategies of dyadic regulation varied, based on what we needed to do to receive our parents' love and avoid rejection. As we aged, while the players changed, the game remained the same. A diagram to depict these strategies might look like this:

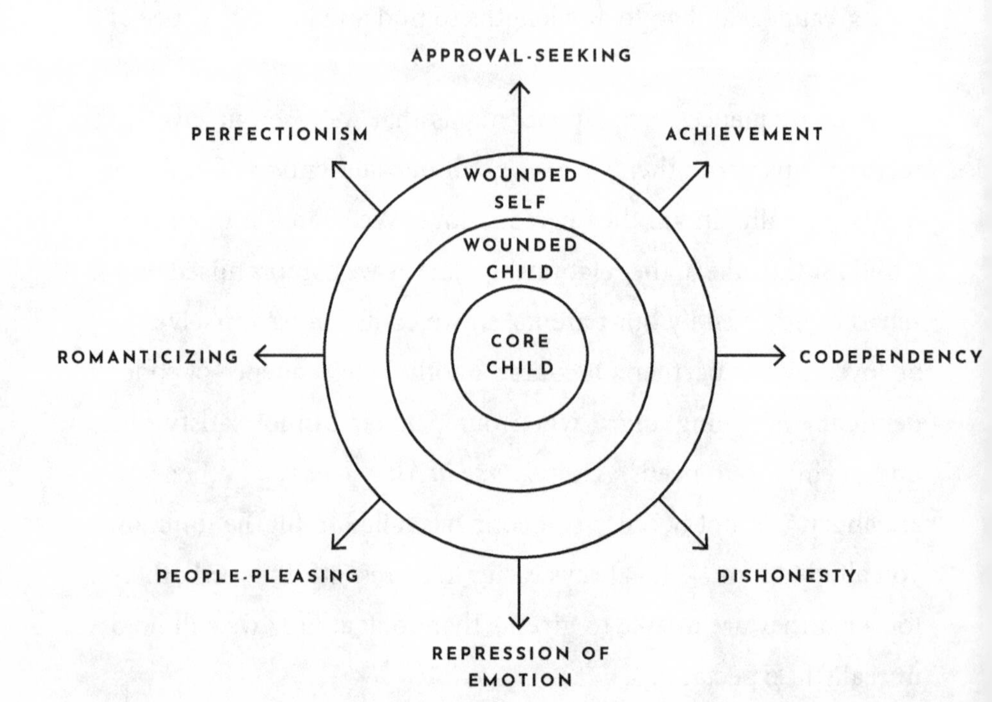

In this diagram, we can see arrows extending outward from the Wounded Self to various strategies of dyadic regulation. The direction of our attention is toward the external world to reduce distress and increase lovability. Such strategies remain a guiding force for many of us as adults. Until we know that we are wholly lovable, regardless of what we *do* as human beings or do *for* other human beings, our Wounded Self will believe that the answer to our problems lies outside of ourselves.

CHAPTER 7

Strategies of the Wounded Self: Autoregulation

In the previous chapter, we saw the various ways our Wounded Self uses dyadic regulation to meet our Inner Child's needs for love and to avoid rejection. However, the intention behind the Wounded Self's use of autoregulation is more oriented toward creating a sense of safety and security for our Inner Child. Objects of attachment are those things that help us to feel safe and secure. If, as children, we had parents who were rejecting and felt unsafe to go to for comfort, we had to resort to other means to relieve our Inner Child's distress.

Without the physiological capacity to regulate our nervous system, we looked to the external environment to meet this need. We transferred what we hoped to receive from our parents onto the inanimate world, so the environment could now give us that feeling of safety and security. The first way we might have experienced this was in relationship with a favorite stuffed animal or toy. Our teddy bear or blanket, for instance, became something that we needed to help us feel okay. We woke up with it, carried it throughout the day, and went to sleep with it. If separated from this object for any length of time, we became scared and distressed. There is nothing maladaptive about this strategy; it was simply the only means we had to feel safe. However, the pattern of our attachment to things outside ourselves can, and often does, become more harmful to us as we age.

ATTACHMENT TO THINGS

As long as we believe that the things of our environment determine our sense of safety and security, we will always need to find something to fill that role. We may spend hours searching for the right phone, computer, coffee maker, shoes, TV, or household accessories. Each object becomes the thing we need to feel okay; it is a grasping from a lack of what we think will help us feel whole. Yet if what we lack is the answer to our wholeness—to our okay-ness—then we will never feel satisfied with what we have.

Related to this is our need for financial security. Money is said to be the "root of all evil," but money is just an object that society has deemed necessary for the purchasing of other objects. When the world of things defines our sense of security, we will naturally become attached to money. How much money we have, how much we are making, how much we're spending, become constant worries. The money in our possession determines how secure we feel, and we become willing to compromise most other aspects of our lives to have enough of it. We may let go of our true passions for a job that offers more financial security. We may forgo quality time with our loved ones to get a pay raise. If we never internalized safety and security from our parents, our Wounded Self will endlessly seek it out in the world of things and money. While there are healthier and more responsible ways to navigate this aspect of adulthood, without having to compromise our needs or those of our family, in our Wounded Self, we cannot see any other options.

DOING AND SELF-SUFFICIENCY

As children with an insecure-avoidant attachment style, we learned that our safety and security were dependent on what we could do for ourselves. If we didn't have parents who were available to help us with daily tasks, such as getting dressed, doing our homework, or making breakfast, we might have felt entirely alone. While it is healthy for a parent to teach their child how to perform certain tasks and then step back to allow them an opportunity for independence, it is very different for a parent to neglect or abandon this role completely. If the latter was our childhood experience, all of our *doing* held an incredible weight of responsibility. If we didn't do it ourselves, it might have never gotten done.

We carry this weight of self-sufficiency and feeling overly responsible into adulthood. Much of our day can be oriented to getting one task done after the next. We check each task off the list in the hopes that it gets smaller, but life's responsibilities seem to keep coming. Once one job is finished, we find another that must be done. Whether it is completing work-related assignments or household chores, we become completely overwhelmed and in the grip of our need for control. Our focus is external, and we in our Wounded Self believe that only when we can manage *all* of our responsibilities perfectly, then we will be safe and life will be easy and comfortable.

In our Wounded Self, we are in the consciousness of our childhood selves, and so all of our childhood beliefs are as real to us as adults as when we were young. Our Wounded Self is overwhelmed by the belief that peace and security can only come from completing all our tasks. Yet our Inner Child is overwhelmed, because when we engage in activities from our Wounded Self, it inevitably results in our abandoning them. We were never taught how to do things mindfully, for whatever needed to be done was often motivated by fear. This communicates to our Inner Child that something is wrong, and without any awareness of our Inner Child's growing distress, we continue to engage in activities to avoid feeling that distress.

Though many of us might attempt to self-regulate through productivity, we may also try through procrastination. Rather than obsessing over our to-do list, we push it out of our awareness, so we no longer feel overwhelmed by it. If, as children, our anxiety didn't motivate us toward doing, it overwhelmed us into inaction. Our Inner Child's threshold for distress was exceeded by our Wounded Self's need for control, and the only strategy left was to avoid doing anything. Yet rather than a conscious choice made by our rational mind, it was the last resort to survive the psychic overwhelm we experienced.

Procrastination may have felt like a more comfortable, less stressful strategy than doing, though it also had its consequences. The more pressure we got from the external world to take responsibility for our lives, the more we resisted, and the more stagnant we became. In adulthood, our strategy of procrastination may be even more pronounced. In addition to increased societal pressures, our Wounded Self internalizes the voice of society, which becomes our very own unforgiving life coach. If we are more prone toward doing, we anxiously listen to the voice and do as we are told. If we are more prone to procrastination, we hear the voice and plug up our ears. Though most societies reward the doer over the procrastinator, both strategies prevent us from living an authentic and inspired life.

CONTROL OF OUR ENVIRONMENT

It is the nature of the Wounded Self to control our external environment to change the state of our internal environment. One way this strategy may have manifested in childhood was in our need to manage and organize our surroundings. When each thing had its place, we felt in control and experienced more peace. As adults this strategy can arise in our need to maintain a rigid organization and cleanliness in our homes, cars, or workplaces. We may notice that whenever we feel distressed we find ourselves rearranging, cleaning, or organizing whatever is out of place. We see clutter, and it makes us feel uncomfortable. Our external environment becomes an externalization of our internal environment so that by putting in order whatever *feels* out of place, we are temporarily relieved. Our experience of relief provides positive reinforcement, and we come to actually believe that the messiness and disorganization of our surroundings are the cause of our distress.

Another way we may have sought to control our external reality was by managing our time. For instance, as a child, we may have woken up with a lot of anxiety in anticipation of the day. If the circumstances and relationships in our lives felt unpredictable and unsafe, we may have found that mapping out the coming day brought a certain comfort. We knew that we would get out of bed, brush our teeth, have breakfast, go to school, attend classes, come home, etc. Even if we couldn't control what happened to us, knowing where we would be and what we would be doing helped ease our Inner Child's distress.

This strategy of planning our day may be very familiar to us as adults. With all the various areas of our lives that are in constant motion, structuring our time helps us manage our distress. The problem is that when things don't go as planned, we can experience overwhelm and panic. Perhaps it takes us longer to get to work than we expected, or certain tasks don't get done. Maybe an unforeseen event requires us to change our plans. When we rely so much on controlling our time, any unexpected shift can throw us off. It is then that the flaws of these strategies come to light.

Another Wounded Self strategy of autoregulation we may have used when we were young was trying to control the objects of our imagination. Perhaps we feared that the boogeyman was in our closet, or there were monsters under our bed. By having our parents check to make sure these imaginations weren't real, we could be put at ease. We may have also adopted ritualistic or superstitious behaviors to create a sense of security for ourselves, such as checking behind the door when entering a room, avoiding the cracks on the sidewalk, or holding our breath when passing a cemetery. The fears that motivated these behaviors, while maybe influenced by a particular movie or story that we heard, came from our Inner Child's feelings of terror and aloneness. By attempting to control these objects of our imagination, we were trying to comfort our Inner Child.

We may come to find, however, that maintaining these forms of control creates more distress than relief. The fear of our Wounded Self is progressive. The more we entertain fearful ideas and act to control them, the more we reinforce the reality of our fears and put patterns of behavior in motion. Whether it is placing items on our desk in a particular order, checking the front door twice to make sure it is locked, or a host of other compulsive behaviors, we are attempting to create a feeling of safety by controlling our external environment. We may be so consumed by our fears and helpless to do anything about them that we become controlled by what we are trying to control.

AVOIDANCE OF INTIMACY

In our dyadic regulation strategy of emotional repression, we were willing to compromise our authenticity to avoid rejection and abandonment. Our parents and peers may have wounded us with their comments and actions but not to such a degree that it felt necessary to relinquish such relationships. However, if the abuse was severe, it may have felt safer to simply avoid contact than risk experiencing further harm. At home, we may have physically isolated ourselves in our rooms to feel out of harm's way or emotionally isolated by making our voices small and presence invisible. If we weren't out in the open and vulnerable, we were less likely to be hurt.

Just as the expression of our authentic selves in our families felt unsafe, so may have been the case for us at school with peers. If we were different from the general crowd, an outlier among those who were deemed admirable, then we experienced some form of abuse. We may have been teased, bullied, picked on, called names, gossiped about, or ostracized. School may have become another place where it wasn't safe to be ourselves. As a result, we were careful to limit our engagement with others, avoiding large groups of people, school clubs, and social events. We chose our friends very carefully and felt comfortable, only having a few.

The pain of our trauma is carried into our relationships today. We may still avoid intimacy, vulnerability, and sharing ourselves with others and limit our engagement in social communities and events. Perhaps we have few friends, if any, outside of our primary relationship, or have been single for a long time. Our trauma is a tape that runs unconsciously in the prospect of any social interaction. Our Wounded Self believes that if we experienced abuse in our past, we could experience it now. And so we close ourselves off from intimacy. We isolate socially and emotionally. When asked how we're doing, we say "good" or "fine"—our go-to responses to keep vulnerability at bay. Our Wounded Self strategies have been with us for so long that we may not even realize that we don't present our authentic selves. Our strategies keep us safe, so we believe, and so we allow them to confine us rather than risk the possibility of more trauma.

When we enter into a relationship with another person, we create a living system that affects our state of regulation. If we have a proclivity toward avoidance strategies, we can often make others the cause of our distress. For instance, when our partner is doing something that threatens our sense of security—such as crossing our boundaries for personal time, asking us to be more vulnerable than we feel comfortable with, or making choices that impact the homeostasis of our relationship—we can react with hostility and blame. We make our distress about them and their actions rather than consider its origin within us. We make their need for connection and quality time the issue rather than look at our own fears about meeting such needs.

• • • • •

A diagram to depict the autoregulation strategies of the Wounded Self could look like this:

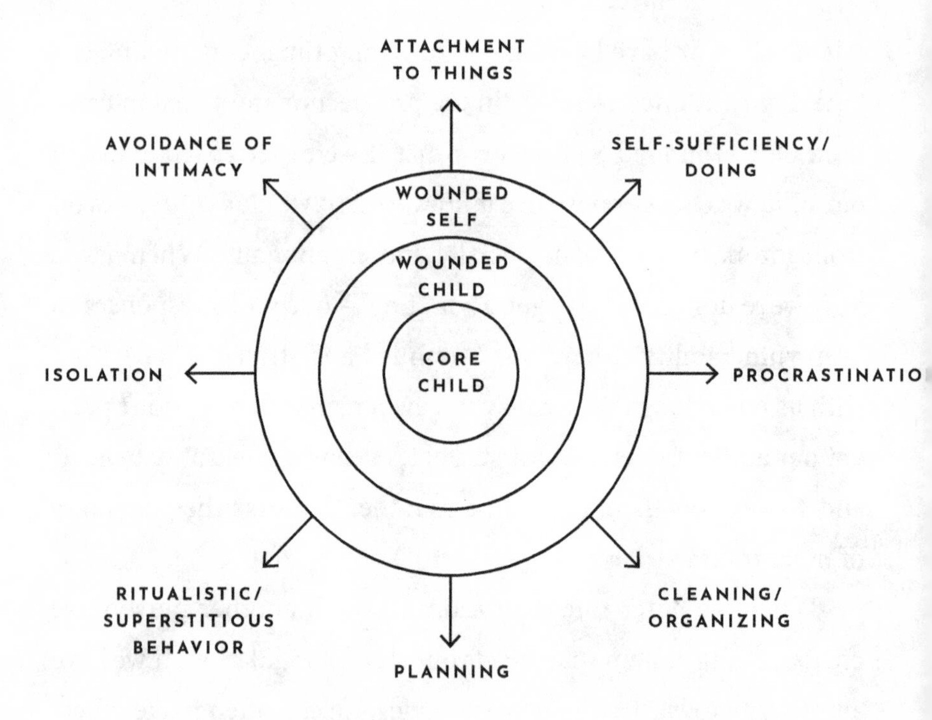

Our Wounded Self strategies of autoregulation seek to control our external reality to decrease our Inner Child's distress. By manipulating our environment or limiting our engagement with it, we create a false sense of personal security.

CHAPTER 8

Strategies of the Wounded Self: Dissociation

Our Wounded Self's use of dyadic and autoregulation strategies served a purpose when we were children. We didn't know how to regulate our Inner Child's distress, and so we continuously looked to the external environment to meet this need. But all of our attempts only resulted in transient moments of feeling lovable or safe, which led to further insecurities. The more we looked outward to change our Inner Child's experience, the more we abandoned our Inner Child in the process.

Every incident of abuse and neglect, every rejection from our parents and peers, are wounds held within the memory of our Inner

Child. When we are without safe and supportive environments to process our suffering, the only remaining strategy is dissociation. Dissociation is used here to describe the conscious and unconscious ways we numb or distract ourselves from the accumulated distress, pain, and trauma of our Inner Child. As children this was the last means by which our Wounded Self sought to cope, and it is a strategy that has become such a part of our culture that we often fail to see how maladaptive and harmful it really is.

Children with an insecure-disorganized/disoriented attachment style, like those observed in the Strange Situation Procedure in Chapter 5, enter states of dissociation involuntarily as a reaction to psychic and emotional overwhelm. Yet if Wounded Self strategies lie on a continuum, used in response to the degree of our distress and the means available to us to moderate it, it may be said that we all engage in strategies of dissociation from time to time to change the way we feel. Involuntary dissociation can be viewed as the most extreme reaction to distress, whereas other strategies, in which we engage in a behavior to alter our experience, are more common in our day-to-day lives.

DISTRACTION

Distraction occurs when we shift our attention away from one thing and onto another, and it is a way in which we, in our Wounded Self, moderate our Inner Child's distress. Our Inner Child exists in our bodies in the form of emotion and somatic sensation, and so when our Inner Child is afraid or in pain, we experience various forms of discomfort. By turning our attention away from discomfort and onto a stimulating alternative, we can avoid feeling. As children, our Inner Child's distress was particularly uncomfortable, because we had little capacity to self-soothe. To cope, we instinctively moved our attention away from our present experience and onto something outside of ourselves. Our Inner Child's distress was apparently diminished not because they were soothed by our actions, but because we cut off our awareness of the distress in our bodies.

The Wounded Self created the universe as a distraction from the Child's original wound, and so this pattern of behavior is deeply rooted in the human condition. Just about everything in the world can be a distraction from the fear and pain of our Inner Child. We learn this as we grow up and are introduced to new toys, games, phones, TV shows, and the Internet. It may have often been the case that our parents introduced us to these mediums of distraction when they could not effectively soothe us. It was much easier to turn on the TV than to turn to us in our distress or to give us ice cream instead of genuine expressions of love. As kids, we had little understanding of our needs, nor means to articulate them, and so when distraction offered us an alternative to what we sought from our parents, we settled.

The lure in distraction was often the stimulation it provided. We developed a proclivity toward excitement. Though we didn't know it, so much of what we used throughout our childhood and adolescence to change the way we felt was used to change our biochemistry. When we were engaged in an exciting activity, it released endorphins or dopamine. We developed attachments to anything that would make our experience more pleasurable, and we continued to engage in these same patterns of behavior as adults. We're not often aware of it, but so much of what we do seeks to induce excitement—not just watching movies, shopping, or playing games on our phone, but also more subtle manifestations of this behavior, like planning vacations, listening to the news, or eating out.

Even without external sources for distraction, our Wounded Self will continuously engage in thinking to avoid our present experience. The part of us that remains in our heads—rewriting the past, wishing for a particular future, concerned with this or that—is our Wounded Self, and what we are doing is avoiding our Inner Child's distress in our bodies. Thinking becomes a habit, a strategy to avoid, escape, or dissociate from the pain and trauma of our Inner Child. Because thinking is often the first way that we seek to escape the present moment, we become well-practiced in this behavior. It feels normal. We become so accustomed to it that we are often unaware that *thinking* is most of our reality. We are not really *here*, experiencing ourselves and the world around us, but are engaged within the world of our thoughts.

ADDICTION

Every time our Inner Child's distress reaches a certain threshold, we engage in some strategy to change how we feel. Yet it is precisely this pattern of behavior that perpetuates their distress and increases our desperation to avoid it. At a certain point, all our attempts to avoid what we are feeling result in suffering that we believe can only be alleviated through mind- and mood-altering substances and behaviors.

Gabor Maté explains:

> *People are susceptible to the addiction process if they have a constant need to fill their minds and bodies with external sources of comfort.... That need expresses a failure of self-regulation.*[56]

While we may think of addiction as something that happens in adulthood, it can often begin at a very early age. If our parents could not relieve us of our distress, or support our capacity to self-regulate, we looked to our environment for alternatives. When we were young, we may have first turned to food, if it was readily available. Eating felt comforting, and so we ate whenever we needed comfort. We came to experience that the absence of distress brought about by food was a pseudo-experience of love. We turned to particular foods throughout the day for self-regulation, and if it worked well enough, our relationship to food became an addiction.

When we grew up, and had more resources, the substances and behaviors we used progressively worked better to meet our needs. While in childhood we may have used food, video games, TV, and movies, in our adolescence we may have used the Internet, social media, pornography, masturbation, sex, shopping, or drugs and alcohol. The more instantly gratifying, the more we were hooked. The substances and behaviors themselves may not have necessarily been unhealthy—it was how we used them, and our intention for using them, that was. As long as the strategies worked, we may have found no reason to give them up. The consequence, however, as anyone who has struggled with addiction knows, is that we became dependent on whatever we used. What first began as occasional use turned to frequent use, and then to chronic use. When we depend on something outside ourselves for regulation, we *need* that something to live and function in the world.

The energy of addiction is that of a child who believes they are alone in their suffering and must, on their own, find any means to escape it. When a child wants something, it is difficult for them to let go of wanting it; the desire becomes fixed in their mind, and nothing but the possession of it can bring relief. When we look to our own experience of addiction, through the lens of the Inner Child, we can see that it is the child in us who cannot let go of what they so desperately desire, even if what they desire is hurting us far more than helping.

While the strategy of using a substance or behavior works at first to numb or change the way we feel, it is only a matter of time before we become enslaved by our addiction. Our Wounded Self becomes so attached to what the addiction offers that the thought of being without it is akin to death. Even when the foundation of our life is crumbling, and the consequences of our addiction are staring us in the face, we may still cling to the false promise it offers and deny our need for change.

SUICIDE

The devastating reality too frequently expressed in the world today is that when all strategies fail to relieve us of our Inner Child's pain, we may look to suicide as a final escape. Lost in the dream of living from our Wounded Self, we believe that only by ending our lives can we be free of suffering. Though this is not the truth, in our despair, it is what we believe, and it is this belief that creates our reality.

The pain that many of us seek to escape is not just that of failed hopes and dreams, or the turmoil of a present circumstance, but a result of our cumulative trauma and abuse. The rejection and abandonment we may have experienced from family, peers, and society can cause unbearable pain. Without the voice and presence of unconditional love that can hold us in our pain and tell us how beautiful and worthy we are, we are left only with what we have been given.

If we find ourselves at this place, lost in the darkness that has become our reality, it doesn't have to end in suicide. Though it may feel like that is the only option left, it is not. When we don't allow the darkness to consume us, it can be a doorway to our awakening. Our Inner Child embodied to experience God's love, and if we can be supported in the time of our greatest need, we can find our way back from darkness into light.

• • • • •

A diagram to depict the dissociative strategies that we may have adopted in our childhood, adolescence, and adulthood might look like this:

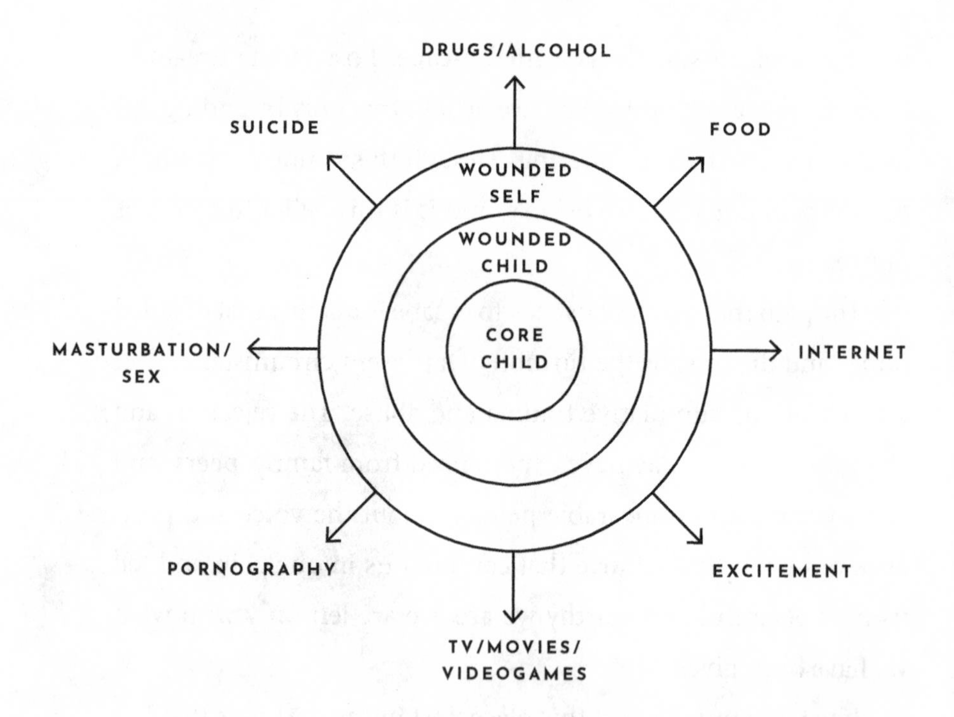

Like the two previous diagrams of Wounded Self regulation, we can see arrows extending outward from the Wounded Self to various forms of dissociative strategies. Each strategy has the same intention: to numb or change the way we feel. While engaging in any particular strategy may create a feeling of peace or comfort, it is really a temporary anesthetic from our Inner Child's pain.

• • • • •

The diagrams of Wounded Self dyadic regulation, autoregulation, and dissociation are separated to show how a particular Wounded Self strategy is motivated by a particular intention. Dyadic regulation is about seeking love, autoregulation is about feeling safe, and dissociation is about avoiding pain. However, many strategies are often motivated by more than one intention. For example, using social media can serve the need for approval (i.e., dyadic regulation) as well as a distraction (i.e., dissociation). Using perfectionism at work can be used to impress our boss (i.e., dyadic regulation) as well as increase our financial security (i.e., autoregulation).

It is how our Wounded Self manifests that distinguishes the "addict" from the "codependent," the "over-eater" from the "hoarder," the "gambler" from the "video-gamer," and the "TV series-binger" from the "workaholic." We take on these strategies to cope with the pain of our life experiences and the messages that told us we're not good enough, lovable enough, or worthy enough.

We can also interpret our Wounded Self's strategies as the impulse to experience God—the source of unconditional love that we sought to experience from the beginning. The Wounded Self seeks what the Child within us seeks, for the Wounded Self is an extension of the Child. But in our Wounded Self, disconnected from the truth of being at one with God, we look to the world for what we believe we don't have: God's love. The goal remains unchanged, but the means we use to find this love, and the things that we believe constitute love are always misguided when motivated by our Wounded Self.

CHAPTER 9

Cumulative Trauma and the Wounded Self

Just because the past has happened doesn't mean it ceases to exist. Our Inner Child and all their memories remain within us as adults, influencing our experience of reality. Part of the phenomenon of the Inner Child is that they experience what we experience whether or not we are conscious that this is happening. An event may take place, a relationship conflict, and we may be present to it or dissociated from it. We may move on quite quickly from the event, as though it was a dream or never really happened, but just because we move on doesn't mean our Inner Child has forgotten it. Our Inner Child is the part of ourselves that is open even when we are closed, that feels even when we are numb, that remembers even when we forget.

Trauma occurs when we are not given a safe and loving environment to allow the emotions of a particular incident to move through us. When our external environment cannot support the expression of our authentic self or the grieving of our trauma, then the layers of our Wounded Self form to protect the vulnerability of our Inner Child. As long as the wounds remain, the existence of our Wounded Self is seen as a necessary defense against abuse from the outside world. As the layers formed, the hurts felt less impactful, not because the abuse failed to reach our Inner Child, but because the defenses of our Wounded Self blocked the impact of the trauma from our consciousness. Yet just because we dissociate from the pain does not mean that the arrows of attack cease to be real.

Our Inner Child is always in direct relationship to us; how they experience reality is determined by how we interpret and communicate it to them. Our Wounded Self's interpretation is influenced by our Wounded Child, the aspect of our Inner Child that is the repository of our trauma, and so we tend to experience life through the lens of our past. Any hurt we experienced in childhood can become an emotional memory that lives within us. If no one helped us feel and process our hurt, then the trauma becomes stored within the consciousness of our Wounded Child.

Our wounds are like a library of books, categorized by the messages we were given, or the type of harm inflicted upon us. Any unhealed wound is activated if a present trigger resembles an experience from our past. What someone says, how they say it, and the context of our relationship are all processed by our Wounded

Self. The comment gets passed through our library of unhealed wounds, and if the right trigger points are hit, it will activate our trauma. All of this happens in the blink of an eye without our conscious awareness. We become the child of our past in the present, feeling just as we did then—hurt, helpless, scared, and alone. How we react to the situation may be similar to how we reacted then. It may only be long after the incident that we reflect upon what took place and wonder, bewildered, what happened.

If relational trauma is understood as the withholding of unconditional love, then the number of events in which retraumatization can occur are limitless. It can show up as low-level anxiety or a crippling force that inhibits our ability to function in the world. How our trauma expresses itself may vary, but the underlying system is the same. It is held within our Wounded Child, buried under the layers of our Wounded Self. Because our trauma is alive within us, it continues to influence our perception and experience of reality.

THE MULTIPLE PARTS OF OUR PSYCHE

As we become aware of our Inner Child and Wounded Self, we realize that our psyche is made up of multiple parts, and that any part can be active at any given time. Each part has its own voice, belief system, perception of reality, and way of surviving in the world. Dissociative Identity Disorder (DID) is a diagnosis given to those who experience having multiple personalities or identities, each distinct from the other, which create an overwhelming amount of distress in the person's life.[57] A common precursor to DID is significant trauma in childhood.[58] When someone with DID is "hijacked" by a particular personality, they lose perspective of any other way of relating to or experiencing the world. When they return to consciousness, they have little to no recollection of what happened. This, in many ways, describes the "Dr. Jekyll and Mr. Hyde" phenomenon of having identities in conflict with one another.

If we examine how we live and engage with the world, we may see that having multiple identities, or states of consciousness, is more common than we think. For instance, if we have experienced addiction, we know the baffling nature by which we are hijacked by the need to get our "fix," despite having the painful awareness that it is the cause of most of our problems. When in the pursuit of our addiction, we lose touch with reality; we let go of what is rational, compromise our values, and take little consideration of how our actions are affecting ourselves and others. We are driven by a force within us that overpowers our decision-making, and we do things that we wouldn't ordinarily do.

A similar phenomenon may occur in romantic relationships. At one moment, we may be spending time with our partner and enjoying each other's company, and in the next moment, we are triggered by something that is said and react from our Wounded Self. We become disconnected from our love for our partner and act in ways that are contrary to how we really feel about them. It may be hours, days, or weeks before we come back to a state of regulation and feel the remorse, guilt, or shame for what we said or did.

The severity of a trigger increases our dysregulation and creates a more solidified Wounded Self state. The more solidified the state, the less flexibility we have to move into a regulated state of consciousness. Additionally, the degree of dysregulation affects how self-aware we are when living from our Wounded Self and how much we remember afterward. If we were never taught tools for self-regulation in response to emotional triggers, then we may be powerless over entering Wounded Self states and powerless to get out of them without substantial help.

CHAPTER 10

Coming Out of Denial

We may have been given many loving messages from our parents growing up, but the hurtful ones weigh heaviest on our souls. On such occasions, our parents' Wounded Selves told us fallacies about ourselves, and because of our innocence and love for our parents, we believed them. In school, we may have been targeted by other Wounded Selves, who judged us, bullied us, and gave us more information about how unlovable we were. We came to perceive ourselves through the eyes of the collective Wounded Self. No one told us or showed us that who we were, despite what others had said and done, was wholly lovable. If we didn't hear this from our parents, from our peers, or from society, we couldn't hear it from ourselves, because we gave so much power to everyone but the voice of God—the voice within us that knows who we really are and how worthy we are of unconditional love.

As adults, in addition to seeking society's approval, we often seek it from our own internalized society. We may live under the control of these messages, and they push us toward perfection and use self-criticism to "help" us. This internalized voice of our Wounded Self is difficult to notice, but we can't miss how our Inner Child feels in response to it. The feeling we get in the pit of our stomach when we do something "wrong." Feeling worthless when we fall short of our expectations. Overwhelm at the sight of an insurmountable to-do list. Shame for not being "good enough." Embarrassment for being ourselves. These are all indications that our Wounded Self has been telling us false truths. Our Inner Child hears the voice of our Wounded Self and believes it, for, without another voice to tell us the truth about ourselves, we are at the mercy of our conditioning.

When we avoid taking responsibility for our Inner Child, we allow our Wounded Self to remain the organizing principle of our psyche—which influences most, if not all, of our thinking, feeling, and behavior. The messages, beliefs, and strategies of our Wounded Self, which formed in our childhood and throughout our lives, continue to guide us in our adulthood. The more we act from our Wounded Self, the harder it is to stop, because our minds become clouded by strategies and false beliefs. We end up feeling disconnected, isolated, and separate from other people. The world feels hostile, relentlessly demanding, and unsympathetic. We lose touch with the sacredness of being vulnerable, honest, and open. We forget who we really are and what is of real value to us, and we step away from the peace, love, and security that God wills for us to experience as eternally present.

As long as we live from our Wounded Self, we are unable to glimpse the reality that lies beyond our fears. Yet, if we are willing to try living another way and turn toward what we've spent our whole lives running away from, we'll discover that what we've been searching for has been here within us all along.

PART III

Becoming a Loving Parent to Our Inner Child

When the world began to unfold and [God] *saw that if it flowed further asunder it would no longer be able to return home to its roots, then* [God] *spoke, "Enough!".... But man too can say "Enough!" to the multiplicity within him. When he collects himself and becomes one, he draws near to the oneness of God.*[59]

—MARTIN BUBER, *THE LEGEND OF THE BAAL-SHEM*

CHAPTER 11

Theology of the Inner Child, Wounded Self, and Loving Parent

We can clearly see the chaos that occurs when we allow our Wounded Self to influence our perception and experience of reality and be the guiding force behind most, if not all, of our decisions. We are not responsible for the pain and abuse we experienced as children. We are not to blame for seeking ways and means to survive, engaging in strategies to cope with our trauma—but as adults, these strategies no longer serve us. Acting from our Wounded Self only perpetuates our suffering; it disconnects us from ourselves and others, and from the real love and peace that is our birthright.

Fortunately, there is another way to live. The archetypes of the Inner Child and Wounded Self are not brought into this world alone. There is also the archetype of the Loving Parent.[60] Our Loving Parent is the part of ourselves that can receive God's love and offer it unconditionally to our Inner Child. It is the part of ourselves that can be guided by God's direction, helping us learn how to free ourselves from the patterns of behavior that keep us stuck.

BECOMING A LOVING PARENT

The story that is ours to claim, of becoming a Loving Parent to our Inner Child and liberating ourselves from the bonds of our human condition, is told in the Book of Exodus.[61] When Moses was born, the Jewish people were enslaved in Egypt. Pharaoh had ordered all Jewish boys to be killed, in fear that one day the Jewish people might become too prolific and powerful and overthrow his rule. To save her newly born son from this decree, Moses's mother placed him in a basket by the bank of the Nile River. Pharaoh's daughter found him, and recognizing him as a Jewish child and taking pity on him, she chose to adopt him as her son.

Moses's parting from his mother is symbolic of the Child who, before the creation of the universe, felt separate from God, and is also symbolic of our own experience when we felt separate from of our parents' love. Moses's adoption is symbolic of when the Wounded Self manifests to "protect" God's Child from feeling abandoned and is also symbolic of when *our* Wounded Self manifests to help us survive the conditions of our childhood. Like Moses, who was raised in Pharaoh's kingdom, and like God's Child, who embodied within the physical universe, so we grow up in the dream spun by the collective Wounded Self. We inherit the "riches" of our society—the chance to reclaim our lovability through the world's approval—but at a cost.

Moses is initially symbolic of the Child, just as we are its divine expression when born into the world. Yet because of trauma and the unloving messages we receive, the Child becomes buried within us, thus creating the Inner Child. For Moses, the Israelites represent his Inner Child. As an adult, Moses witnessed the oppression and enslavement of his own people under Pharaoh's rule, just as we become aware of our Inner Child's conditions under the management of our Wounded Self. The act of Moses killing an Egyptian who was beating an Israelite may be akin to our initial attempt to take back ownership of our lives. Yet like Moses, who recognizes the futility of his actions and so flees, we too come to find that the power and habitual nature of our Wounded Self cannot be overturned by our own volition.

As an adult, Moses left the life he was accustomed to and became a stranger in a new land, just as we, upon realizing the nature of our conditioning, enter a new awareness that is both confusing and frightening. Yet it was there in the desert where Moses experienced the presence of God. The archetype of the Loving Parent was awakened in him as a result, because the Loving Parent is given life through God. Moses was instructed by God to free his people from Pharaoh's rule, but overwhelmed by the responsibility of such a task, he didn't know how he could do as God asked. And so God assured Moses that he would not be alone, that God would be with him; it would not be Moses who spoke or acted but rather God through him, so that, from God, Moses was given the power to free his people and return to the Promised Land.

When we enter into the desert of our own spiritual life, we are made ready to receive the Presence of God, and the experience is no less transformative for us than it was for Moses. We hear the call to become a Loving Parent to our Inner Child, to free ourselves from the wounds of our past and habits of our present, and to return to the reality that is truly ours. The prospect of what is asked of us may be impossible to conceive of, but when we recognize that we are not alone in what we do—that God is with us—then we too are given the courage to embark on this journey.

Freeing his people from Pharaoh's rule didn't happen immediately or easily for Moses. He had to prove his power to Pharaoh, and only after performing a series of miraculous feats did Pharaoh finally agree to let Moses's people go. Similarly, becoming a Loving Parent to our Inner Child requires that we prove to our Wounded Self that we are capable. Our Wounded Self is obstinate, not because of malice, but because of fear. They perceive the present through the trauma of our past, and so believe that they play a vital role in our continued survival. Until we can demonstrate our ability to be a Loving Parent to our Inner Child, our Wounded Self will be hard-pressed to let go of control.

Living from our Wounded Self for so long has built a seemingly insurmountable barrier to a new way of life. We become so attached to our Wounded Self strategies that opening to the vulnerability of healing is like walking into the Red Sea. Without trust in God's care for us and without feeling God's presence guiding us, we believe that to step into these waters will drown us and that returning to our old way of life—to Egypt—is much safer. Yet when the Israelites expressed such fears to Moses, he reassured them of God's unconditional love—that what looked like certain death was, in fact, the passage to freedom. They trusted in what Moses told them, and the Red Sea parted, and "Thus the Lord delivered Israel that day from the Egyptians."[62]

Like Moses and the Israelites, we'll come to find that our journey of recovery isn't made of one impasse, but many. It is not made of one miracle which takes us closer to the Promised Land, but many. Time and time again, we are confronted with the reality of our conditioning, the wounds of our past, and the fears that arise when we are asked to change. But as we go forward, we discover that God is with us, and we are given the courage needed to heal.

GUIDANCE FOR THE WAY

Another archetypal story that offers guidance for our healing path is the life of Jesus. Like Moses, Jesus is initially symbolic of the Child. The mythical story of his birth, of having been given to Mary from God rather than conceived by natural means, is similar to what happens with our Inner Child. On a metaphysical level, our Inner Child is given to us from God to love unconditionally so that by our love, the Child's manifestation within our consciousness may transform ourselves and the world. It is perhaps no coincidence that Jesus came as a light into the world during the darkest time of year, just as the awareness of our Inner Child comes as a light during the darkest time of our lives.

Becoming a Loving Parent to our Inner Child is perhaps the most challenging task we are asked to do as human beings. It may be said that even Mary had anxieties at the prospect of being a parent, to which the angel Gabriel replied, "With God nothing shall be impossible."[63] Gabriel's response to Mary is also a response for us when we feel overwhelmed by the task of being a Loving Parent. Though this gift may at first feel like a burden, we come to experience it as the birth of a new, awakened reality. Encouraged by our faith that God is with us, we too, like Mary, may proclaim, "Behold, I am the servant of the Lord; let it be to me according to your word."[64]

As Jesus is symbolic of the Child, so Mary and Joseph are symbolic of his Loving Parent, embodying both the masculine and feminine qualities that are the expression of God's love. Just as the Child was created in God's image, both masculine and feminine, so the Child's manifestation within our consciousness created *our* dual nature. As a Loving Parent, regardless of our gender, we are given the ability to manifest the total expression of God's love. Though Mary and Joseph's parenting style is scarcely mentioned in the New Testament, we can infer based on the influence that parents have on their child's development that they played an integral part in supporting Jesus to become who he was. The building blocks from which we learn to parent ourselves come from our own parents.

It may be said that the Loving Parent was awakened in Jesus in his adulthood during his baptism, when "the heavens were opened to him, and he saw the Spirit of God descending like a dove and coming to rest on him."[65] The teachings of Jesus's ministry—of unconditional love, compassion, acceptance, and forgiveness—are how we are asked to be a Loving Parent to our Inner Child. The sick and injured, the outcast and dejected, the blind and disabled (mentioned in the Gospels), are all expressions of our Wounded Child, who had suffered the pains of society's oppression and abuse. The tax collectors and sinners, the prostitutes and transgressors, and the Roman soldiers and Pharisees are all expressions of our Wounded Self (also mentioned in the Gospels). Yet they too are treated by Jesus in ways that tell them of their worth and lovability.

If Jesus is symbolic of our Loving Parent, then we, too, are given the means to embody God's unconditional love. When we can show our Inner Child who they really are and come into relationship with others in ways that reflect their holiness, then we have become who we are meant to be. The destiny, as it was given to Moses, and the prophecy, as it was given to Jesus, are both ours. That is our opportunity and blessing as human beings.

CHAPTER 12

The Inherent Instinct of Our Loving Parent

While we may have lived much of our lives from our Wounded Self, there have also been times when we have lived from our authenticity, from the part of ourselves that emerges when we allow our experience to find expression. As children, though we may have used playthings in our environment for distraction, we may have also unknowingly externalized our Inner Child in relationship with them. We became a parent to our Inner Child through our own stuffed animal or doll, comforting and helping our Inner Child feel safe enough to share their feelings. By giving them voice and expression through our objects of attachment, we could experience emotional regulation. Despite being unconscious of the deeper processes taking place, we had the inherent instinct to love and heal ourselves.

Projecting our internal reality onto our playthings diminished the overwhelm of our experience and helped us come into relationship with it. While the ways we parented our Inner Child may have been modeled after our parents, containing expressions of love, as well as fear and control, our instinct to love them unconditionally was also present. Our playthings held much more meaning and purpose than just that of inanimate objects; we gave them animation and life through imagination and intent.

PROCESSING EMOTIONS THROUGH PLAY AND THE ARTS

We may have also used our toys to process confusing and painful circumstances. With action figures, we may have played out the story of "good guys" versus "bad guys," expressing our feelings about the injustices we experienced in our family or at school. If we didn't know how to communicate our feelings or felt it unsafe to do so, we found another way. The violence we dramatized through our action figures was an expression of our own pain and anger, and the victory of good against evil was the hope we carried—that one day we might experience the love, peace, and safety we yearned for.

In our childhood and adolescence, our inherent instinct to be a Loving Parent to our Inner Child may have also found expression through the arts. We discovered that visual art, dance, music, and theatre could all be modalities to communicate our Inner Child's thoughts and feelings. The language of the arts felt safe for us because we didn't need to speak our story with words; we could paint our story, dance our story, and sing our story. In the honest expression of ourselves, we were unknowingly supporting our Inner Child's voice, allowing our long-held emotions an opportunity to breathe and live beyond the walls of our conditioning. We gave expression to not just the pain and trauma of our Wounded Child but the joy, curiosity, and playfulness of our Core Child, which may have also been repressed by the culture of our family and society.

The environments in which we engaged in the arts were often supportive of our authentic selves. We were with others who also had the desire to express themselves and a teacher who encouraged our expression. Though our Wounded Self may still have been active at times by comparing ourselves with others, wanting to be the "best," or competing for the attention of our teacher, the intention of the environment itself diminished the intensity of these strategies. Ultimately, we engaged in such communities because we wanted to be there—our Inner Child wanted to be there. The arts may have been one of our only reprieves, and its impact left an indelible impression.

Living as an adult in society often strips us of the ways we can support our Inner Child's life and expression. The demands of work, family, fitting in, and getting by all seem to take precedence over the Child within us. We are constantly moving against the stream of the collective Wounded Self that pushes us to live in the ways of distraction, addiction, codependency, achievement, and attachment to the external world. We all have the inherent instinct to be a Loving Parent to our Inner Child, but if we do not fan this precious spark within us, it may very well be buried under all the "stuff" we fill our lives with. A natural instinct must be consciously supported for it to grow into its grandest possibility.

CHAPTER 13

Connection with God, the Source of Unconditional Love

Becoming a Loving Parent to our Inner Child is a process that begins with awareness. We come to see how we have been guided by our Wounded Self and controlled by conditioning and habit. In our startling awakening to what has become our life, we may try to stop and turn back upstream, counteracting the tendencies we have supported thus far. But we will likely find that such attempts are futile. Though we may have been raised to believe that self-sufficiency is the way to get things done, it is not so in the process of our healing. The power of our Wounded Self, when left to run amok, is unstoppable. We may try in every possible way to overpower it—adopting new routines, diets, exercises, and therapies—but it cannot be done, not without a Power greater than our Wounded Self.

The power that enables us to be a Loving Parent to our Inner Child is God, but for God to work in our lives, we must create space for God's presence. If we are in active addiction or dependent upon a substance or behavior, it will be nearly impossible to make space for God, let alone our Inner Child. Our only concerns will be the maintenance of our habits. What's important is that we allow God to do for us what we haven't been able to do for ourselves and seek out the necessary help from others to support us in this process. The miracle that occurs when our desire to continue an addiction or other dependence is relieved can profoundly awaken us to the reality of God. Though this is only the beginning of our journey toward healing, it is a monumental event.

Despite the miracle that lifts us out of our denial and into an awareness of something greater than ourselves, we may still resist the idea of coming into relationship with God. Yet it is not really God that we are resisting, but our idea of God—the idea given to us by our families, society, and religion. As children, just as we were vulnerable to the messages of our families and peers, so were we vulnerable to the messages of religion. This isn't to say that religion is inherently traumatizing; it is rather how people use religion to control others. At the core of religion is the teaching of unconditional love, but these original teachings are often distorted or lost to us. As decades, centuries, and millennia pass, we become more and more distant from them and adopt the teachings of the Wounded Self.

When we surrender our discernment that comes from the heart, we are vulnerable to accepting the religious messages we hear as truth, whether or not they feel loving or true. Growing up, we may not have been given any choice about attending religious services or being a part of a religious community. Any rebellion or resistance may have resulted in negative consequences. So we were forced to take in the false messages about God and ourselves that religion presented. Without being given a choice, the God of our family became our God, and we lost touch with the organic and personal nature by which God enters our understanding and experience. If the religious abuse we experienced wasn't enough to make us run away from the idea of God, then we may have been afraid to explore any understanding of God that was contrary to what we were taught as children.

Both scenarios cut us away from the source that is the foundation of our healing. To either reject God completely or to believe in a punishing and judgmental God prevents us from experiencing the love of God that is given to us unconditionally. If we look at the Judeo-Christian religions, for instance, it is easy to see how human fear and control have been projected onto God. Rather than us being made "in the image of God,"[66] it is God who is made in the image of our humanity. God then becomes the controlling parent of our childhood, using conditional love to shape and mold our behavior, and we become the "unworthy" children of God, who are never good enough to receive God's love.

For our relationship with God to be of value, we may need to rewrite our understanding of God. We may need to not only let go of the idea of God that was given to us by religion, but also anything which is a projection of our parents' attitudes and behaviors. For instance, if it wasn't safe for us to express ourselves honestly with our parents, we may believe that it's not safe for us to do so with God. If we experienced our parents as emotionally or physically distant, we might believe that God is also distant. If our parents only showed their love for us when we were "good," we may not believe that God will love us when we are "bad." As long as we believe God to be the figure given to us by religion or the projected image of our parents, we will invariably distance ourselves from relationship with God, because that relationship engenders fear and shame instead of intimacy and vulnerability.

CREATING A NEW IMAGE OF GOD

We must come to believe that God is far more than the ideas we were given, and that God's love for us is unlike anything we have ever experienced. To do this, we must create an image of God in our imagination that is as close to the truth as possible. And so we can start by believing that God's love is unconditional, that God exists in every moment of our lives, that God is always present and available, and that God is always listening to our hearts and offering us support and guidance in return. We can start there, and let this idea of God become a reality. Day by day, we can allow our understanding of God to transform into something truly magnificent, for the possibility of God is only as limited as our ideas.

Ultimately, we want God to be more than just an idea but a source from which we can live and breathe. We want God to be a direct experience, for only then can it be grounded and have permanence in our lives. When we make the experience of God something unattainable, something that only "holy" people can have, then we are selling ourselves short. We all can have our own "burning bush" experience, but it may not be as sudden or immediately transformative. Our awareness of and relationship with God will more likely occur gradually, and when it happens in this way, it is more likely to be real, sustainable, and ever-deepening.

How we choose to connect with God may look different for each of us. The action we take may be prayer, meditation, walking in nature, mindful breathing, conscious movement, chanting, a ritual of some kind, or whatever else feels right. What is most important is our intention. We are seeking to open to God's love and presence to embody our experience more fully. From this place of being consciously connected with God, we are better able to have a relationship with our Inner Child.

Connecting with God is a practice, and just like any practice, the more we do it, the more it becomes a part of our daily routine. We may, however, feel resistant to making this choice regularly. If the practice is new, then it may feel strange, vulnerable, or ambiguous. We might not really know what to do or how to do it. We might not feel anything in particular when we connect with God, and because it doesn't provide immediate results, we may question whether it is "working." This is all normal. What's important is to keep on practicing and have faith that, over time, the relationship that we truly desire with God will manifest. One thing is for sure: when we take action to consciously connect with God, we are not doing it alone. Just as God is always with us in our lives, whether or not we are conscious of it, God is also with us in our practice of deepening our relationship with God. If we can let ourselves be guided, we are sure to be led in a way that will allow the practice to grow.

The healing power of God's love is not conditionally given—it is a power that is patiently waiting for us to say "YES" to our healing. The decision is *ours*, but our ability to make this decision consistently takes time, for learning how to love ourselves unconditionally takes time. God's love is the unconditional love that we offer to our Inner Child. It is not a separate love; it is simply Love, no matter what the context. We are offered this opportunity as human beings to realize our oneness with God through choosing to love our Inner Child as God loves us. As we build a relationship with our Inner Child, we build a relationship with the inherent part of ourselves that feels separate from and abandoned by God. As we become a Loving Parent to our Inner Child, we become the bridge between our Inner Child and God; we become the vessel for God's love so that by our unconditional love, we teach our Inner Child that they are a Child of God.

CHAPTER 14

Becoming a Loving Parent to Our Wounded Child

Our Inner Child is a psycho-spiritual structure within our consciousness that is made up of three distinct sub-structures: Our Wounded Self, Wounded Child, and Core Child. Our Wounded Self becomes our default state of mind, the scared child of our youth who believes that their worth, lovability, and sense of security are dependent upon what they can do in the world and how they are judged by others. When we are living from our Wounded Self, we cannot make any distinction between the sub-structures of our Inner Child. All we experience are the anxieties, frustrations, and dissatisfactions of our daily life, which we believe to be solely due to our environment. If we experience more severe emotional states, we write them off as symptoms to be diagnosed and medicated. From the consciousness of our Wounded Self, we cannot be a Loving Parent to our Inner Child; we are living *as* a child who is trying to parent itself. It is only when our consciousness can expand beyond enmeshment with our Wounded Self—beyond fear—that we can come into relationship with our Inner Child.

Through our relationship with God, we can cultivate the structure of the Loving Parent within our consciousness. This structure is separate from that of our Inner Child and therefore enables us to both witness and be present to our Inner Child's experience without being enmeshed. When entering into conscious relationship with our Inner Child, we'll find it most helpful to be in connection with each aspect, because our embodiment as a human being and experience of trauma has disintegrated the whole, unified structure of our Inner Child into separate parts. Though our Wounded Self, Wounded Child, and Core Child are all connected, without a Loving Parent, they exist in conflict with one another, much like siblings who have been left home alone. The Wounded Self takes on the role of "parent," but cannot lovingly parent themselves or their siblings for they are just a child. To be a Loving Parent is to come into relationship with each aspect of our Inner Child, so that by our love, the Child that was split can become whole again.

Our relationship with our Inner Child is similar to one a parent has with their child. While the dynamic may appear different, because we as a Loving Parent are in relationship with three distinct aspects of our Inner Child, these aspects are also naturally a part of the human child. We just don't normally consider the presentation of a child's mood and behavior as the manifestation of a particular personality.

Like the parent-child relationship, our relationship to our Inner Child can be characterized by attachment styles. An important awareness, however, is that it is our Wounded Child's met or unmet needs that determine the nature of our attachment relationship. Similar to what occurs for infants, when our Wounded Child feels rejected or neglected by us, it creates an insecure attachment, which provokes the manifestation of our Wounded Self strategies. Then our Wounded Self runs the show, and our Wounded Child remains isolated and abandoned within us. When we as a Loving Parent can meet our Wounded Child's needs for safety and love, it creates a secure attachment, which allows for our Core Child to be expressed. Therefore, our initial aim is to become a Loving Parent to our Wounded Child, for it is this relationship that is the doorway to healing.

INSECURE-DISORGANIZED/DISORIENTED ATTACHMENT

How we relate to our Wounded Child and Inner Child, in general, is influenced by how our parents related to us. Through their conditional love, we learned what sort of behavior and modes of expression were permissible and which ones weren't. We internalize these messages and unconsciously perpetuate them with our

Wounded Child. And so in many ways, the attachment styles we had with our parents form the basis of our attachment relationship with our Wounded Child. For instance, we will initially experience our Wounded Child in our bodies as distress, for just as the infant communicates their unmet needs from distress, so does our Wounded Child. If, when we were children, our distress was invalidated, minimized, belittled, or ignored by our parents, then the expression of our Wounded Child's distress may trigger these same reactions in us.

Another way we may have adopted our parent's behavior and mirror it in relationship to our Wounded Child is in the degree of importance we place upon meeting their needs versus fulfilling the wants and desires of our Wounded Self. Our parents are often our most influential role models, and so we learned what to prioritize in our lives based on their behavior. If work, achievement, approval from others, or strategies of dissociation took priority over helping us feel safe and loved, then we are likely to carry these same values and tendencies into the relationship with our Wounded Child.

Our attachment relationship with our Wounded Child is determined by how well we can meet their needs for security and love. Before coming into relationship with God, we are living primarily from our Wounded Self, perpetuating our Wounded Child's feelings of rejection and abandonment through our use of strategies. We numb or desensitize ourselves to our Wounded Child's distress or attribute it to circumstances beyond our influence. We take little to no responsibility for our experience. How we act toward our Wounded Child at this stage of the relationship is similar to parents whose child has an insecure-disorganized/disoriented attachment style. Though we may exhibit "ordinary" behavior according to society's norms, our chronic use of strategies is self-abusive, disconnecting us further and further from the experience of our Wounded Child. Our Wounded Self's dissociation in reaction to trauma has become our own experience of "normal." We are living in a dream-like state yet unaware of any alternative. It is only when we begin to wake up that we realize we have actually been dreaming.

Before cultivating our Loving Parent in connection to God, we may have had an awareness of our Wounded Child but were unable to act outside of the influence of our Wounded Self. This state of self-awareness, which we can call our "Adult," surrounds our Inner Child but has no power of its own to make changes in our behavior, much like Moses before his awakening in the desert. A diagram to depict what our consciousness would look like at this initial stage of our recovery is this:

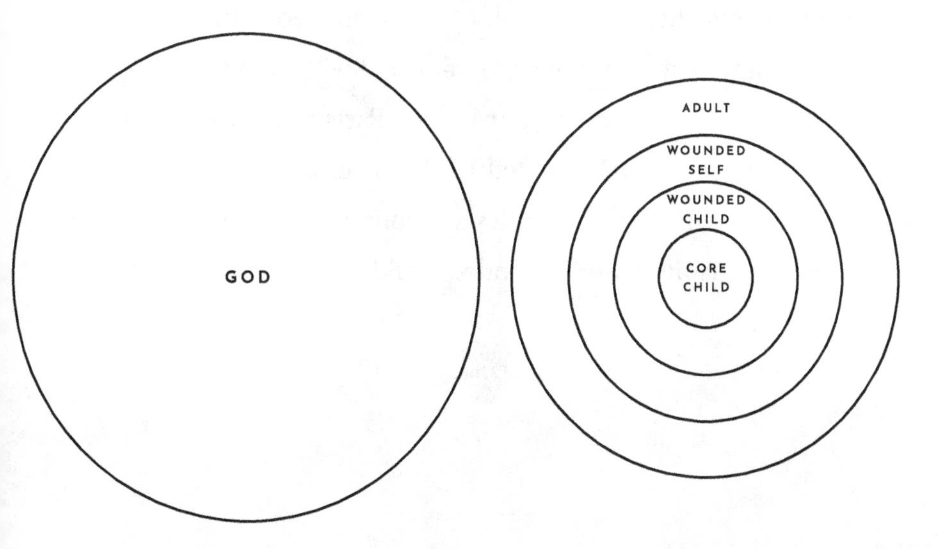

In the diagram, we can see God, as represented by the large circle, and our Adult that surrounds the three aspects of our Inner Child. The circle that is God does not represent any limitation of God's existence in space or time but only our awareness of and felt connection with it. Without a connection to God, we live from the consciousness of our Wounded Self and continue to engage in strategies of dyadic regulation, autoregulation, and dissociation to survive. Though we may have an awareness of our condition (as indicated by our Adult), we are helpless to move out of it. Our Loving Parent has not yet manifested, and our relationship to our Wounded Child is characterized by an insecure-disorganized/disoriented attachment style.

INSECURE-AVOIDANT ATTACHMENT

Through our connection with God, we can cultivate the Loving Parent within our consciousness, which is given the power to make loving choices on behalf of our Wounded Child. The degree to which we feel aware of and connected with God will determine how established we are in our Loving Parent and how capable we are of meeting our Wounded Child's needs. A diagram to show how our Loving Parent manifests in connection with God and how our relationship to our Wounded Child changes, as a result, looks like this:

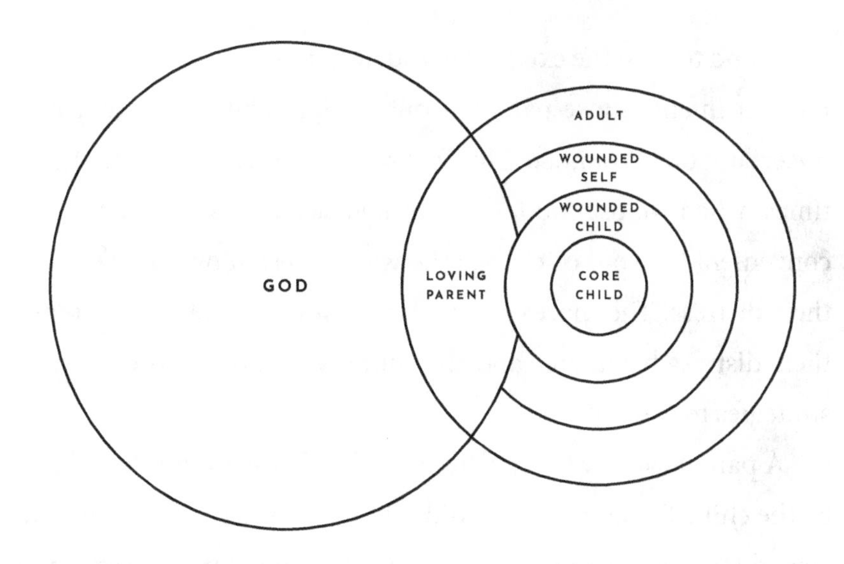

In the diagram, we can see God, our Adult (which surrounds our Inner Child), and our Loving Parent (which is created by the part of our Adult that is merged with God). Whatever proportion of our Adult lies outside the circle of God is completely influenced by our Wounded Self. However, even at this early stage of connection with God, our capacity to be a Loving Parent to our Wounded Child is greater than it was before. As a result, we move out of an insecure-disorganized/disoriented attachment relationship and into an insecure-avoidant attachment relationship. Though most of our decisions are still made from our Wounded Self, we are no longer operating in complete denial or ignorance of our Wounded Child.

An infant depends upon their parent to regulate their nervous system's activity, and similarly, our Wounded Child depends upon us to regulate theirs. When our Wounded Self's fears about our security and lovability direct our attention away from our Wounded

Child and toward the external world, it causes us to abandon them. Like an infant whose parent is out of sight and whose return is uncertain, our Wounded Child's distress skyrockets. During these times, when we use food, the Internet, sex, drugs, or whatever is convenient to avoid or change the way we feel, it only exacerbates their distress. The more we avoid our Wounded Child, the more their distress heightens, and the more we continue to engage in strategies to avoid it.

A parent's ability to regulate their child's distress is internalized by the child. So if our parents did little to help us regulate when we were distressed, then we are essentially beginning from the ground up. Therefore at this stage of our recovery, our capacity to tolerate our Wounded Child's distress is limited. Not only do we lack the practice of being present to our experience, but our connection with God—the source that enables us to courageously and compassionately do so—is minimal. Consequently, it becomes easy for us to resent our Wounded Child and perceive them as a nuisance; our awareness of them in our bodies doesn't engender compassion but loathing. And so our attitude and behavior toward them are much like a parent whose child has an insecure-avoidant attachment style. We resent how our Wounded Child interferes with our lives, are unresponsive to their signals, and avoid being present to them in their distress.

To have an awareness of our Wounded Child changes how we are asked to live. Our mindless pursuit of activities and strategies now brings with them the emotional impact of such decisions. When we make choices that are in conflict with our Wounded

Child's needs, we feel their pain, and though we may continue to act in disregard of it, our experience is tinged with the color of their suffering.

We are *always* in relationship with our Wounded Child, whether we like it or not. When we perceive our Wounded Child as some problem to be fixed, symptom to be medicated, or pain we wish to be rid of, our Wounded Child feels it. Just as the child with an insecure-avoidant attachment style distances themselves from their parents to avoid the pain of chronic rejection and abandonment, so does our Wounded Child do with us. Our Wounded Child has their own consciousness and responds to our behavior. When we act in ways that feel unloving, they distance themselves from us on an emotional and somatic level. Their distress may be the only expression they feel safe enough to reveal, yet that too may become diminished. When we don't create safety for them to exist, then they don't share themselves with us. Such disconnection perpetuates our Wounded Child's trauma and maintains an internal system of dysfunction that cannot support our healing.

• • • • •

Over time we come to see how our choices directly affect our Wounded Child and our relationship with them. When we live from our Wounded Self, we are disconnected from the power of God within us and are unable to act from our Loving Parent. We lose the ability to choose between what is truly loving for ourselves and what is not. When our awareness of God's presence in our lives is minimal, we will inevitably be overpowered by our Wounded

Self's fears and need for control. To become a Loving Parent, we need to be conscious of the choices we make daily, moving away from those that perpetuate our Wounded Child's feelings of rejection and abandonment and toward those that honor them and feel loving. To do this, however, we must be in collaboration with God, for the more we can rely on the security that this relationship offers, the more we can embody God's love in relationship with our Wounded Child.

The journey of becoming a Loving Parent to our Wounded Child and building a secure attachment with them is two-fold: we are simultaneously deepening our relationship with God while deepening our relationship with our Wounded Child. Though initially, it is the former that supports the latter, over time, we'll find that each relationship supports the development of the other. That is the miracle of what we are cultivating.

At first, being in relationship with God can feel just as uncomfortable and ambiguous as being in relationship with our Wounded Child. Without concrete evidence, we may still doubt God's existence. It is important to note, however, that the results that concretize our belief in God are often influenced by that very belief. For instance, if in prayer we "pay lip service", like a child who was told to pray by their parent instead of genuinely feeling moved to pray, then our experience in prayer and of God will be fruitless; it will be as notable as talking to a wall. But if we pray because something within us tells us that the universe is more than just matter but is infused with the energy and consciousness of God, then our experience can be something very special. Sometimes all we need is that one experience to catapult into an ongoing relationship with God. At other times our Wounded Self's argument against the existence of God counteracts the inkling of our belief. Yet if we are determined to increase our belief in the reality of God and build a relationship, then we just keep trying as best we can to ignite that spark.

There is great wisdom in cultivating a discipline of spiritual practice, making the time every day to pray, meditate, or seek conscious contact with God in whatever way feels right. We're not only creating new habits but also making room for the experience of God. The more times throughout the day we can appoint for this relationship, the better our chances are for feeling the results of our practice. How we each come to experience God will be unique, but some shared qualities may be feelings of peace, reassurance, hope, surrender, grounding, warmth, love, stability, and ease. Such experiences, however, may take time to unfold. When our consciousness is dominated by the energy and content of our Wounded Self, it is challenging to open to the presence of God that is here and now. But every time we do experience glimpses of God's presence, it reinforces our belief, which motivates our action to continue seeking connection.

INSECURE-AMBIVALENT ATTACHMENT

Through deepening our relationship with God, our Loving Parent becomes more accessible in our decision-making. Yet, because our Wounded Self occupies much of our consciousness, our ability to meet our Wounded Child's needs for love and security is still quite limited. A diagram to show what the makeup of our consciousness may look like at this point is this:

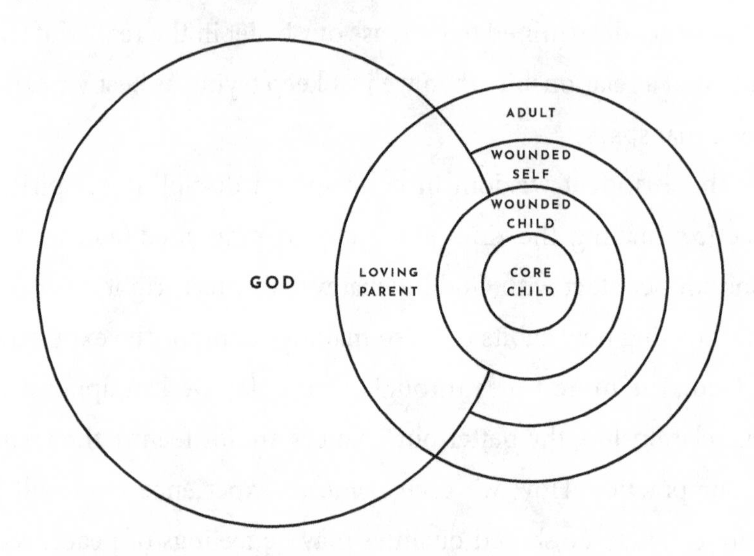

Our behavior toward our Wounded Child at this stage of relationship will be most characteristic of parents whose infants have an insecure-ambivalent attachment style. Our external life remains our primary focus, and our relationship to our Wounded Child is secondary. Though we may at times acknowledge our Wounded Child's distress, our attempts to soothe them are half-hearted; we do so only when it is convenient for us or when the discomfort of their distress in our bodies is severe enough. We take whatever time is sufficient to calm our Wounded Child and then return to our to-do list. It is this dynamic that perpetuates our Wounded Child's insecure-ambivalent attachment style. Our increased attempts to meet their needs offer the promise of relief, but the result leaves them chronically frustrated.

This pattern of relationship is not sustainable. When we frantically move throughout the day motivated by strategies of dyadic regulation and autoregulation, we not only pass over opportunities to be present to our Wounded Child but give them the message that they are unimportant. Being a Loving Parent does not mean that we must forego our adult responsibilities or refrain from activities that we enjoy, but that we are conscious of the choices we make, for it is in *how* we live that most affects our Wounded Child. As long as our attachment to the world remains as it's been, we are apt to continue experiencing our Wounded Child as a nuisance. The soothing of their distress is only a means to an end; we do it as though removing an obstacle in our way rather than from love. We do not see the blessing of our Wounded Child and of being in relationship with them, yet we also can't easily return to being ignorant of them as we were. We can either stay where we are, feeling a victim to a condition we never asked for, or we can learn how to love our Wounded Child and experience its transformative results.

• • • • •

Similar to an infant's crying, our Wounded Child's distress is a signal for our attention. As a result of our increased willingness to acknowledge our Wounded Child in our lives, we ironically feel more of their distress. Though this can be quite uncomfortable, it is actually a good sign. Feeling our Wounded Child's distress means that they feel safe enough to signal to us, and when we are more sensitive to their signals, we can more readily respond to meet their needs.

When our Wounded Child's attachment behavior is activated, and we experience their distress, what they most need is for us to be present to them and their experience. Therefore, whenever we feel their distress, our first step is to recognize that whatever we are doing or how we are doing it is not working. Our actions have not been helping our Wounded Child to feel safe and loved. Yet simply stopping our behavior is difficult, for our Wounded Self is motivating the actions that have caused us to abandon our Wounded Child, and they will not easily let go of control. Our Wounded Self is driven by the influence of society, believing that our sense of security and lovability is contingent upon what we do in the world and how "successful" we are. Achieving these ends, according to our Wounded Self, doesn't come from mindfully engaging in activities, taking breaks, or feeling our feelings. No, all of this takes too much time—time that could be better devoted toward doing the things that are of "real" value. When we are not consciously connected to God, our Wounded Self's fears become *our* fears, and their argument for doing whatever we are doing is very convincing.

During such times, to lovingly respond to our Wounded Child's distress, we need to reconnect with God. Sometimes the best we can do when caught in the grip of our Wounded Self's fear and need for control is to just ask God for help. That may be enough. The power of humility goes a long way, for just as it was our humility that opened the door to a relationship with God, it is our humility that allows God to help us when we are in need. Another action we can take is to share with God our fear in stopping whatever activity we are doing and of the dreaded outcome we believe will occur if we do. We may also find it helpful to take some conscious breaths and allow God's love and support to enter us. What's most important is that we turn our attention, if even momentarily, away from whatever we are doing and toward the source that will enable us to become a Loving Parent toward our Wounded Child.

As children, the intensity and overwhelm of our distress was too much to be present to on our own. Without a parent to help us feel our feelings, we resorted to using strategies to cope and survive. This is the same dynamic that is created when we abandon our Wounded Child in their distress and allow our Wounded Self to make decisions for us. To diminish our compulsion to engage in those strategies, we need to learn how to be present to our Wounded Child, because when they feel supported and loved the strategies of our Wounded Self cease to control our lives.

Conscious contact with God gives us a greater capacity to be in relationship with our Wounded Child. What is so challenging about feeling distressed is the energy of it. It surges through our body, tightens our muscles, constricts our breathing, and persists until it is given some form of release. In our Wounded Self, we are in the habit of making that release something that works in the moment, but which often has long-term consequences. When we can recognize our distress as a signal from our Wounded Child, we can transform our beliefs about it. Compassion arises when we humanize our distress—when we see the face of our Wounded Child in their experience. Something that may help to achieve this is bringing to mind an image of our childhood selves, either from a photo that we have or from our imagination. In our minds, we construct an image of our Wounded Child so that our relationship with them becomes multidimensional. We feel them with our hearts, and we see them in our minds. We may also try placing our hands wherever we feel their distress in our bodies. It is as though we are embracing them with love when we hold ourselves in this way. This action may be enough to calm our Wounded Child's distress and can be a powerful tool in deepening our relationship with them.

Below are some steps to help you begin responding to your Wounded Child's distress:

1. If you feel distress in your body, it is likely a signal from your Wounded Child and an indication that you are doing something that is causing you to reject or abandon them.
2. After noticing your Wounded Child's distress, take time to connect with God in whatever way feels most helpful (e.g., prayer, meditation, mindful breathing, conscious movement, etc.). This will enable you to step into the consciousness of your Loving Parent.
3. If you still feel resistance toward your Wounded Child, try bringing to mind an image of yourself as a child (from a photo or your imagination) or placing your hands over wherever you feel their distress in your body.
4. Take time to just be present with what you feel, breathing naturally, and allowing the tension in your body to find its natural release. Through this action of turning toward

> your Wounded Child and embracing them with love, you are helping them to feel safe and cared for.

As we are learning to become a Loving Parent, it normally takes a while to calm our Wounded Child's distress. Just as infants with an insecure-ambivalent attachment style are slow to be soothed,[67] so will be the case with our Wounded Child. They do not yet trust our accessibility and responsiveness. But the more we show up in relationship to them, the more they will come to trust our ability to meet their needs. Over time, through making choices, again and again, to be a Loving Parent and acting in ways that assuage our Wounded Child's doubts, we create the foundation for a secure attachment.

CHAPTER 15

Secure Attachment with Our Wounded Child

The more conscious we are in daily life, the more we can include our Wounded Child in it, and the less distress they experience. When we are more responsive, they are easily soothed by our efforts to comfort them and will begin to express more varied forms of communication. Though up to this point we have primarily felt our Wounded Child in our bodies as distress, they are much more. When we help our Wounded Child to feel safe and loved, we create a container that allows for deeper layers of their emotional experience to be revealed.

FEELING OUR WOUNDED CHILD'S EMOTIONS

Emotions can often feel uncomfortable because we were never taught how to relate to them. If we have been in the habit of repressing our emotions, or locking them away in some dark cellar, we are repeating the neglect and abuse our Wounded Child experienced when growing up. When we reject the expression of our Wounded Child, we are parenting ourselves the same way in which we were parented and reinforcing the message that having emotions are unacceptable.

What we often label as "emotional discomfort" is really just the experience of our Wounded Child and our incapacity to be present to it. Working with our Wounded Child's emotions is in many ways working with the trauma of unmet needs—of not having been given love or safety; of feeling rejected and abandoned. These are the deeper emotions, held beneath the more superficial expression of distress, and they too ask to be held with compassion and presence.

To be a Loving Parent means to not only have an awareness of what our Wounded Child is feeling but to *feel* what they are feeling. Because living from our Wounded Self has disconnected us from our bodies, it may take a while to become aware of where we feel our Wounded Child's emotions. With practice, we'll find that we can most readily feel our Wounded Child in our belly, sternum, and chest. The activation of a specific location often corresponds to a particular set of emotions. For example, the chest houses our Wounded Child's grief, the sternum our anxiety, and the belly their feelings of abandonment and rejection. However, where we feel our Wounded Child's emotions may be unique to each of us and will become more apparent over time.

We cannot start by swinging open the door to emotion, because that, in the mind of our Wounded Self, would open the door to trauma, and they will quickly create a wall of resistance to avoid drowning in it. Our Wounded Self's fear of trauma is the very fear that created the universe as a distraction from the original wound—from feeling abandoned by God. Such a strategy will remain active if we try to jump headfirst into feeling our Wounded Child's emotions. Unless the process of feeling our emotions is gradual, our Wounded Self will engage in any strategy to avoid it. Therefore, the next step to feeling our Wounded Child's emotions is to reconnect with God. Through conscious contact with God, we experience the safety and security within ourselves to feel our feelings without the need to protect against them. God is our lifejacket when we fear we will drown in our emotions. God is our flashlight, guiding us safely into the darkness of our experience. We allow the presence of God to be within us and come to internalize the safety and security that it offers.

When we feel grounded in God's love and support, we can turn toward our Wounded Child's experience from our Loving Parent. Our Wounded Child is perceptive about our motives, and when they feel our intention to support them, they begin to show up more on an emotional and somatic level. Our loving actions offer them a new message: that their emotions are important, that their experience is important, and that *they* are important. Our demonstration of love for our Wounded Child dissolves their outer shell, and we become more aware of the emotions underneath. As our intention changes from distraction and dissociation to feeling our feelings, we begin to experience more of our Wounded Child.

Living disconnected from our Wounded Child is very traumatic for them. As we turn toward their experience, we begin to feel the emotional impact of our past behavior. Just as a child would feel anger and grief about having been neglected or forgotten, so does our Wounded Child, and so anger and grief may be the first noticeable emotions. What is critical is to allow such emotions to be as they are. Their appearance is a sign that our Wounded Child feels safe enough to show us how they feel, and allowing their expression is the most loving thing we can do. To the best of our ability, we try to stay with our Wounded Child's experience, letting go of all other concerns. We experience the energy, the tension, the moving of anxiety, anger, and grief, the tightening and opening of our chest and face, and the releasing of our Wounded Child's tears.

• • • • •

We've covered a lot of ground, so here is a recap of the steps you can take to begin feeling your Wounded Child's emotions:

1. Notice where in your body you feel your Wounded Child's activation (key areas include the chest, sternum, and stomach).
2. Reconnect with God, using whatever practices feel right for you (e.g., prayer, meditation, mindful breathing, conscious movement, etc.).

3. Connect with your intention to bring love and compassion to your Wounded Child.
4. When you feel ready, turn your attention toward your Wounded Child in your body. Notice the sensations and emotions that are present (e.g., distress, grief, anger, aloneness, etc.).
5. Take time to just be present with your experience without trying to fix or change it. Allow the sensations and emotions to move naturally—breathing, feeling, and holding your Wounded Child with love.

With practice, we come to realize that when we can feel and compassionately hold the energy and emotions of our Wounded Child, we no longer have to abandon them.

Unlike the Wounded Self, whose strategies direct our attention away from our Wounded Child, the direction of our Loving Parent's attention is inward, toward our Wounded Child. A diagram to illustrate this is below:

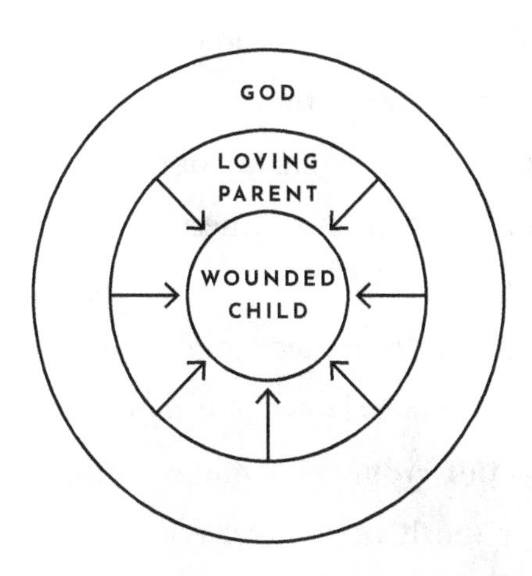

In the diagram, we see God as the outermost circle, our Loving Parent within the circle of God, and our Wounded Child within the circle of our Loving Parent. (Our Wounded Self and Core Child are left out of the diagram to show that our attention is placed solely on our Wounded Child.) When we feel held in God's love, it enables us to hold our Wounded Child's experience from that same love. The arrows in the diagram show the direction of our Loving Parent's attention. When we are fully present to our Wounded Child's experience, it encourages their emotional expression.

DIALOGUING WITH OUR WOUNDED CHILD

We have become familiar with relating to our Wounded Child in our bodies by recognizing their signals of distress and supporting their emotional expression. However, to stop here would mean to be in relationship with only part of the phenomenon that is our Wounded Child. We can also talk with them. If we believe in the presence of our Wounded Child, then we can hear their voice. Often, we may only recognize the loud, constant chattering of our Wounded Self, drowning out the small, quiet voice of our Wounded Child. It takes practice to make room for and encourage their communication, but the more earnestly we show up and try, the easier it becomes.

Speaking with our Wounded Child is similar to speaking with another person; it is an exchange of listening and responding. The difference is that our Wounded Child is within our consciousness and requires our sensitivity to create a space in which they feel comfortable communicating and expressing themselves. What is most important is our intention. If we truly desire to hear our Wounded Child speak, learn about their experience, and support the expression of their truth, it will help them feel safe enough to do so. If our attempts are intended as a quick fix to relieve our distress or to change how we feel—an intention motivated by our Wounded Self—our Wounded Child won't feel safe enough to speak. We must be willing to drop our agendas and enter into the liminal space in which our relationship to our Wounded Child takes on a miraculous new form.

Helping our Wounded Child speak also requires us to use our imagination. It is not about making up what our Wounded Child says, though it may feel like this at first; it is that we embody the voice and experience of our Wounded Child present in our bodies. Our Wounded Child's experience has a story, a reason for its existence. We may intellectually know why we feel the way we do and list the various causes, but that doesn't allow our Wounded Child to tell us how *they* feel. Our Wounded Child often knows much more about our experience than we do, because it goes much deeper than intellectual understanding. Whatever activates a particular emotional response in us has also affected our Wounded Child, and what we feel is usually *their* response to what has happened, more than our own. When we open the door of verbal communication and ask them about their experience, what they tell us can shed a lot of light on why we feel the way we do.

Here are some steps you can take to begin dialoguing with your Wounded Child:

1. When you are aware of having a particular emotion, turn your attention toward your Wounded Child and place a hand wherever you feel them.
2. Just as you did when relating to them nonverbally, try to maintain an attentive, compassionate presence.
3. If it is helpful, you can bring to mind an image of yourself as a child, expressing the emotion that you are feeling. Notice what happens as you hold your Wounded Child in your mind's eye.
4. Focus only on being present to them and their experience, as though they were your own living child. It is this attitude and intention that is reflective of unconditional love, and which creates a deep connection with them.

When you have established a connection, then you can begin by speaking to your Wounded Child. Doing so is similar to speaking with a human child. We want to be sensitive to the words we use to create a safe space that supports their authentic communication. At the same time, we want our words to arise naturally—less from our minds and more from our hearts. You can start by acknowledging your Wounded Child in some way and asking them how they are feeling. Whether something has happened that has upset them (be it your own behavior, someone else's, or a certain situation), as well as what they are needing from you to feel safe and loved. You may already know what you're feeling, and why, but asking questions and listening to the answers allows your Wounded Child to tell you these things from their own experience. Something that can facilitate your Wounded Child's communication is to adjust your posture and alter the pitch and tone of your voice to better reflect theirs. Again, rather than forcing it, allow these alterations to arise naturally. Though it will likely feel awkward at first, giving your Wounded Child as much expression as possible allows them to exist in their fullest.

A conversation between our Loving Parent and Wounded Child might sound like this:

> **Loving Parent:** *Hi, my child.... It's so nice to be here with you. Are you feeling anxious?*
>
> **Wounded Child:** *Yeah.... I feel scared. (While our Wounded Child might respond with words from the get-go, it's also possible they respond by nodding, which we can feel internally. We may also find that our Wounded Child speaks using a language reflective of their age, as illustrated here, using the word, "scared," as opposed to "anxious.")*
>
> **Loving Parent:** *I hear that you're feeling scared.... What's feeling scary for you? (Reflecting back to our Wounded Child what they say can help them feel heard.)*
>
> **Wounded Child:** *I feel scared that you're going to leave me when you go to work. I don't want to be left alone.*
>
> **Loving Parent:** *Is there something I can do to help you feel more connected with me when I go to work?*
>
> **Wounded Child:** *Can you take more breaks? And take time*

to be with me and breathe together? I feel scared and overwhelmed when you do so much and forget about me.

Loving Parent: *I'm so sorry that I forget about you when I go to work. I will try to take more breaks and breathe with you. Thank you for sharing with me how you're feeling and what you need from me.*

It takes a lot of courage to engage in a dialogue with our Wounded Child, especially when we choose to embody their voice and experience. Our Wounded Self may feel especially self-conscious and embarrassed about engaging in this practice because of how "strange" it might seem to others. The only people we way may have ever seen talking to themselves out loud are those whom society has judged as "crazy." The difference is that we are *choosing* to engage in verbal dialogue to support connection with our Wounded Child. To help our Wounded Self feel comfortable enough to do this practice, we can find a private, quiet place that will allow us to have a more focused, undisturbed conversation with our Wounded Child.

ADDITIONAL PRACTICES

Two additional practices that can encourage verbal communication with your Wounded Child are written dialogue and using props. The practice of written dialogue with your Wounded Child can look very similar to the process described above and can even support it. For instance, when dialoguing, you may find it challenging to maintain your attention as you shift back and forth between your Loving Parent and Wounded Child. The thread of content can get jumbled, and the energy of emotion that arises can disconnect you from the present moment. During such times, choosing to use written dialogue can help you manage your level of emotional activation and maintain your focus. Conveniently, it also allows you to record any important information discussed.

A technique that can support your written dialogue is using non-dominant handwriting. In this practice, let your Wounded Child communicate through your non-dominant hand. While it may feel a little funny (and take longer to write), doing so can help you speak less from your rational, left brain, and more from your creative, right brain. If this doesn't work for you, it is still very possible to speak from your Wounded Child using your dominant hand. Additionally, using different colored pens to indicate your Loving Parent and Wounded Child can help you more easily identify which communication is from whom.

Similar to what you may have unknowingly done when you were young, using a stuffed animal or doll to stand in for your Wounded Child can help you externalize their voice and experience, as well as create a more palpable connection with them. When you practice dialoguing with a prop you can simply hold it in your arms and allow the conversation with your Wounded Child to occur as it normally would. Or you can try turning your prop to face you when you speak to your Wounded Child and turn it away from you (but against your body) when speaking *from* your Wounded Child. This can help create distinction between your

Loving Parent's and Wounded Child's communication, as well as facilitate smoother transitions between the two.

A benefit of this practice is that whatever you choose to be the externalization of your Wounded Child is something that you can use as often as you like, and wherever you like. You can even let your Wounded Child choose the stuffed animal or doll they wish to represent; it may have nostalgic value or portray certain characteristics that embody the essence of who they are.

The more we communicate with our Wounded Child, the more comfortable it will become for them and us. Creating a daily practice, such as taking time every morning to "check in," can increase our Wounded Child's feeling of safety and engender an easier flow of communication. Like other aspects of our relationship, regular practice will make communication more effective. The more we dialogue, the more peace we will feel throughout the day, which is a reflection of our Wounded Child's experience—of feeling heard and seen, safe and loved. Through this practice, our Wounded Child becomes real—not just an idea or concept, but a living reality.

MAINTAINING CONSISTENCY AND INTENTION

Becoming a Loving Parent to our Wounded Child is a process; it doesn't happen overnight. Often, we can make headway in building a conscious relationship with our Wounded Child, and then life happens, responsibilities build, and we prioritize other tasks. When we then try to reconnect with our Wounded Child, it can feel as though we are back to square one; it's harder to feel the nuances of their experience, and dialoguing feels forced. Such instances remind us that, like any, our relationship with our Wounded Child requires dedication and consistency. When we leave, they leave; when we show up, they show up. Because our Wounded Child has a consciousness distinct from our own, they are always responding to the choices we make and the way we live. Though lapses in connection can feel threatening, we'll find that our deepening attachment can withstand periods of separation if we take the time to reconnect and repair.

While it is ultimately our love for our Wounded Child that will build a secure attachment, our increasing sensitivity to their distress can motivate us to respond to their needs more quickly. However, if during these times we don't take steps to be present to our Wounded Child's experience, our Wounded Self gains power, both in their influence over our decision-making as well in decreasing our sensitivity to our Wounded Child's distress. We become number to the subtleties of our Wounded Child's attachment behavior, which permits us to continue acting from our Wounded Self uninterrupted. When we don't feel our Wounded Child, we need to accurately assess whether it is the result of our increased connection to them or disconnection from them. The former calms our Wounded Child's distress, but the latter desensitizes us to it. Just because we don't feel our Wounded Child doesn't necessarily mean their needs have been met.

Something else to be mindful of is how our increased sensitivity can make us vulnerable to being overwhelmed by our Wounded Child's distress. Because we are still growing our capacity to be present to our Wounded Child, when a circumstance overwhelms our ability to soothe them, we can experience symptoms of dissociation. These can include disorientation, difficulty focusing our attention, feeling inundated by our environment, and confusion. Although such symptoms may feel alarming, they are only an indication that we have abandoned our Wounded Child; the improved quality of our attachment relationship has just made us more sensitive to feeling it.

We may experience this form of dissociation when we engage in Wounded Self strategies, when our Wounded Child's trauma is triggered by an interaction or situation, or when we avoid emotional intimacy with them. For instance, when we take time to be present to our Wounded Child and support their emotional expression and then suddenly shift our attention away from them, it can immediately activate their attachment behavior. Their reaction is similar to an infant, who, after being held by their parent, is abruptly put down; the intensity of our Wounded Child's protest can feel overwhelming and cause dissociation. As we build a secure attachment with our Wounded Child, we need to be careful about how we make these transitions. Our Wounded Child is still learning whether they can depend on us, and though this doesn't require our continuous, undivided attention, it does require a conscious effort to help them feel safe. One way we can make transitions easier is by allowing our contact to find its natural place of completion, communicate what we will be doing next, and learn how we can help our Wounded Child feel connected as we go about the rest of the day. When we follow up on our Wounded

Child's request with action, it promotes a greater sense of trust in the relationship.

• • • • •

As our relationship to our Wounded Child deepens, we find it is easier to let go of old patterns of behavior. Our motivation for change not only comes from the pain of neglecting our Wounded Child's needs but from our growing desire to make this relationship more of a priority. We come to genuinely love our Wounded Child, and this carries us forward. Over time we learn how to orient our day in ways that help them feel connected with us. Like an infant, our Wounded Child needs routine and predictability. When we make a daily commitment to spend time dialoguing, feeling what is present, and expressing our love for them, it helps our Wounded Child feel more securely attached as we go about the rest of our day.

Though routine is effective, it isn't a foolproof plan for moderating our Wounded Child's distress. Sometimes we feel their activation when it isn't so convenient—we're at work, spending time with our partner, or hanging out with friends—but we need to learn how to navigate these situations without neglecting or abandoning our Wounded Child. If we are doing something, we may find that simply acknowledging them may be enough. Other times, we may need to create more space for them to tell us how they're feeling. Regardless of what specific steps we take, when we can show up with unconditional love, we'll find that our efforts go a long way.

How consistently we act from our Loving Parent will fluctuate, but our parenting doesn't need to be perfect to create a secure attachment. Through struggle and success, we foster a conscious relationship with our Wounded Child in which they feel safe enough to communicate and express themselves, and in which we feel courageous enough to show up. This is a miracle and is evidence of how far we have come. A diagram to depict what our relationship with our Wounded Child and God might look like at this stage of our recovery is this:

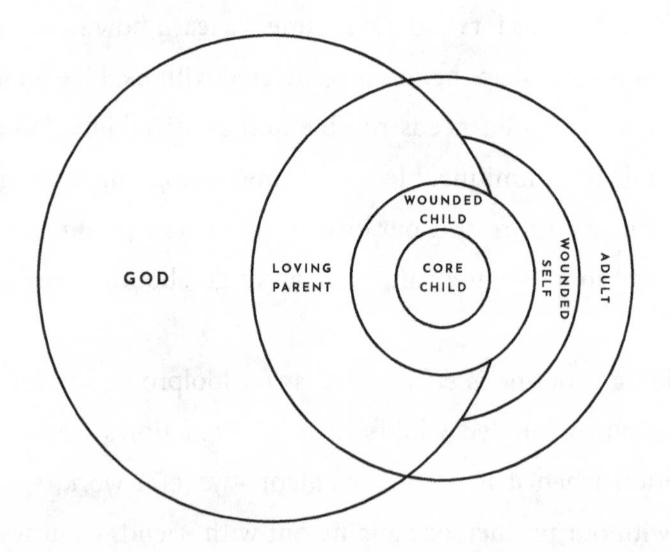

As our relationship with our Wounded Child becomes more secure, so does our relationship with God. This is not always a conscious process, and often the loving actions that have become our norm are the result of *feeling* God's presence more than knowing it. Whenever we make choices on behalf of our Wounded Child, we demonstrate our trust in God's care for us. The courage to love what is present, to dialogue with what cannot be seen, to feel what we have resisted for so long, are all indications that God is working in our lives and that we are allowing it. The result, as the diagram shows, is that our Loving Parent begins to occupy more space in our consciousness than our Wounded Self. Though we will, at times, continue to make decisions from our Wounded Self, our actions are more often guided by love than fear.

Because God has become more of a presence in our lives, we are given the power of *choice*. Whereas previously, we may have been conscious of our decisions but felt powerless to act any differently, today, we have a greater ability to respond to our Wounded Child's needs from our Loving Parent. We are no longer driven by the misguided strategies of our Wounded Self. We come to understand that it is not what we do in the world that determines our sense of security and lovability, but how we show up for our Wounded Child.

CHAPTER 16

Healing the Trauma of Our Wounded Child

Trauma is not just the result of abuse or neglect, but of being left without support to process it. Though we may not have had such support when we were young, we can provide it now. The safety we create in the present with our Wounded Child gives them permission to share their suffering, and as we listen and understand, their long-held pain is given rest.

We want this healing work with our Wounded Child to be organic; we want it to *not* be "work." When we make the healing of our Wounded Child's trauma into a project, we are entering the process from our Wounded Self. We will either resist it to avoid our Wounded Child's pain or will overlook the very sanctity of the process itself. Moreover, our Wounded Child will not feel safe to share their trauma with us if they sense our ulterior motives. Therefore, whenever we are aware of our Wounded Self's motivations, it is simply time to reconnect with God. In God, we are reminded that there is no need to rush, that our healing is not a checklist to complete and be done with, but that where we are and where we're heading can be a beautiful unfolding into unconditional love.

• • • • •

Being in relationship with our Wounded Child means being in relationship to their trauma. As we become more practiced in dialoguing and feeling their feelings, we'll find that most occasions when our Wounded Child is in pain are opportunities to heal the wounds that have been activated by our present circumstance. Because much of our trauma happened in relationships with others, we'll find that on any given day, when interacting with our partner, friends, family, or employer, there will be something that triggers us. A trigger is the activation of a wound, and the particular event that triggers us, be it something someone says or does, often holds the same content, energy, or intention as that of the original wounding. For example, if we receive criticism from our employer, it may activate our trauma of having never felt good enough for our parent's love or of having never measured up to their expectations. If someone makes a joke about our appearance or behavior, it may remind us of an incident from childhood when we were bullied or picked on by peers. We'll often find that what feels most wounding are incidents that trigger our past experiences of rejection and abandonment.

In many regards, trauma work is grief work; in our trauma was the loss of unconditional love, security, connection, and innocence, and much of our healing comes from simply grieving these losses. In our loving presence, we allow God to correct the false beliefs that we created long ago about ourselves, beliefs held within our consciousness as truth, but which we come to realize are illusions. Our trauma is real, but the messages we were given in our abuse are not. When we can show up for our Wounded Child as the memories of our past trauma resurface, support the expression of their grief and whatever other emotions arise, and validate the reality of what occurred and how painful it was—and still is—we can begin to heal. We offer our Wounded Child a corrective experience when we reassure them through our unconditional love that who they are is not who they were taught they are.

TRAUMA WORK IN PRACTICE

When your trauma is activated during the day, it is not always possible to process it with your Wounded Child in the moment; and where you are and what you're doing may have very well been the catalyst for your experience. However, the sooner you can create conditions for being present to your Wounded Child's trauma, the better. If you feel resistance toward engaging in this work it is helpful to first reconnect with God. Allow God's love and presence to bolster your courage to be a Loving Parent to your Wounded Child.

When you feel ready, you can turn toward your Wounded Child's experience in your body and hold them in the energy and emotion of what's arisen. Establishing a connection in this way helps your Wounded Child to feel safe and secure, and therefore more comfortable with communicating the content of their activation. You can then make space for your Wounded Child to speak and give voice to their words as they arise from their experience. For example, if you feel their fear and anxiety, they might say, "I feel scared"; if you feel their grief and loss, they might say, "I feel sad." As mentioned in the previous chapter, your Wounded Child's voice and the words they choose to express themselves can often be reflective of a child's vocabulary, for they are speaking to you from a young age. Let them say whatever they need to, however they need to. Just listen, and where it feels right, you can reflect back what you're hearing and empathize with their experience. If your intention is to truly learn and understand what's present for your Wounded Child, then you will naturally communicate your sincerity and desire to support them. This will deepen your connection and allow for more fluid exchange.

As you learn about what incident activated your Wounded Child's trauma, you can ask if it reminded them of an experience when they were young. A particular memory or image may come to mind, and this can often be a form of communication from your Wounded Child. Feel what arises in response to the memory or image and remain open to whatever they want to tell you about it or whatever emotions want to be expressed. You can ask if they were given a certain message from that experience, such as having done something "wrong," or having been told that they were "bad," and again, allow them to communicate whatever they need to. Listen, and hold them in what arises. Through your love, you can rewrite the story they were given about themselves during that time. If you can look at whatever trauma occurred through the eyes of your Loving Parent, then you can reassure your Wounded Child of their innocence, worth, and lovability.

As we create a womb for our Wounded Child that offers unconditional safety and support, we'll experience the grief and trauma of our past surfacing more easily. Our memories will become more accessible, almost as though our Wounded Child were offering them as opportunities for connection and healing. Everyday occurrences may give rise to emotion; the book we are reading, the movie we are watching, the parent who we see lovingly tend to their child's needs, all can move us in ways that we previously were unaffected by. When we become more awake to our Wounded Child, our past will find mirrors in the present. Our ability to remain connected to them in the expression of what arises is what keeps the door of communication open.

OUR WOUNDED SELF'S RESISTANCE

The practice of turning toward our Wounded Child's trauma isn't easy. What is most challenging, aside from feeling the magnitude and intensity of our emotions, is working with our Wounded Self's resistance. We may find that we are only able to dip into our grief and pain briefly before our Wounded Self pulls us away through some form of distraction. One moment we are with our Wounded Child, comforting them, crying with them, and the next moment we are lost in some fantasy or story completely unrelated to the process we were just in.

Our Wounded Self can make us believe that there are more important things to do than healing our Wounded Child's trauma. Their argument may be so convincing, in fact, that we engage in self-abandonment in the midst of self-love. This can occur at any time in our processing. For instance, if our to-do list comes to mind as we are feeling our Wounded Child's pain, it is likely a strategy of our Wounded Self to distract us from where we are. If this happens, we can simply notice the urgency of our thoughts, take a moment to breathe and connect with our intention, and turn back toward our Wounded Child.

Our Wounded Self's resistance may also arise after our pain has transformed into peace, but before our time with our Wounded Child has come to its natural completion. Once the immediacy of our pain is relieved we return to our day. When we do this, however, we may only be touching the surface of the wound and not truly healing it. Therefore, if we're quick to move out of conscious contact with our Wounded Child after feeling emotional relief, we need to carefully assess our motivation.

SURRENDERING TO THE PROCESS

Not all thoughts or impulses that arise during trauma work are from our Wounded Self. Sometimes an image may come to mind that speaks to us, helping us connect to the root of our trauma or to the experience beneath the image. Rather than a distraction, it is an entryway. While what occurs may seem random or unrelated to where we are, if we can entertain its deeper significance and allow our imagination to guide us, it can give rise to understanding or emotion that we may not have experienced otherwise.

Over time, as we engage in this work, it will become more organic and spontaneous, like a river that flows effortlessly through all sorts of terrain. We listen, we feel, we breathe, we connect with God, we deepen our connection with our Wounded Child, and so on. We cannot predict what each occasion will look like or what may arise, but if we enter with trust, we are sure to be led where we need to go. The more we can let go into the process of our healing, the less struggle we will experience, and we will come to find that surrendering is actually quite pleasurable. In the course of healing our Wounded Child's trauma, we experience God's infinite love; we rest in it—marinate in it—until it is God, not ourselves, who tells us it is finished.

It's important to allow the process of healing to be what it is and not force it or seek to control it. We need to trust that whatever is happening, whatever arises, whatever is revealed or not revealed, completed, or left unfinished, is just as it is supposed to be. If we can believe that God is present and is guiding us in this process, then we come to trust that all will be healed in its own time. We may believe that freedom from suffering can only come from healing every trauma—every incident where we were wounded in a particular way. What we come to experience, however, is that simply living in a conscious, loving connection with our Wounded Child is healing in itself. That is the gift we are given.

CHAPTER 17

Deepening Our Trust

Recovery can feel like a journey of moving alone in the dark. It is difficult to believe that God is there in the unknown, waiting for us beyond the edge of our discomfort. So often, we don't venture out into what we haven't experienced because we fear it may overwhelm us or cause unending pain. Yet it is the decision to walk into the unknown that leads to our liberation. We experience glimpses of this when we take risks in our recovery, when we turn toward our Wounded Child's distress instead of avoiding it, or when we choose to express our grief instead of pushing it away. But even after experiencing the rewards in taking such risks, we may still be terrified of doing so. We stand at the gateway like Moses at the Red Sea, questioning whether we will be given safe passage when we let go. If we do not venture beyond the question, we cannot experience the answer.

God is a part of this journey of recovery. It is God that is helping us come to believe in God's care for us, and it's as simple as letting go bit by bit and trusting in the results. Only after letting go can we experience how we are cared for. With each experience, we build evidence that supports our belief. Though at times we may feel lost in confusion, fear, and habit, we don't remain there as long as we used to. Something in us moves us toward sanity, empowering us to let go and ask for help. The strength to continue moving forward, even with apparent setbacks and bouts of hopelessness and doubt, is the strength given to us from God. God wants us to succeed and know all that we have been given.

Coming to believe in God's care for us is a process of removing the doubt that has hidden the truth from our awareness. With each experience that shows us the ground beneath us is stable—that God is here and supporting us—our faith turns to trust. Trust is our internalization of the truth; it is the result of allowing God to teach us of God's presence. The more we surrender, the more God sinks into our being, and the less we fear taking risks for our recovery. Yet this internalization requires our daily effort. No matter how long we've been at it, each day is a new day and asks us to reaffirm our trust in God. Through morning prayer and meditation, walks in nature, or participation in a spiritual community, we rededicate ourselves to the practices we've been cultivating. Over time our knowledge of God's presence moves to a level that is deeper than our worldly consciousness, down into the spiritual interiority of our being. Though life may not always give us what we want or what is comfortable, we trust that regardless of our circumstances, all will be well.

The more we trust in God's care for us, the more courage we have to be a Loving Parent to our Inner Child. Yet, in our daily efforts, we can forget that God is *our* loving parent and wills for us to know how much we are loved. We can be so focused on trying to meet our Inner Child's needs that we don't stop to rest and receive nourishment. Our practice of prayer and meditation becomes a means to an end—a way to fill up our tank so we can continue doing the hard work that recovery requires. But God also wants us to rest, as on the Sabbath that was created on the seventh day.[68] The purpose of the Sabbath is for making time to commune with God, letting that be enough. We don't need to *do* anything; we are just asked to be God's child and to receive God's love. This is important; it reminds us that life is just as much about receiving as it is about giving.

Making time for spiritual rest feeds us in ways that no other practice can, and we can do this as often as we like. If we were to only rest and receive God's love one day of the week, we might find ourselves burning out quickly. But if we take the time every day to commune and rest in God, and let that be our only intention, then we'll find ourselves renewed with life and the capacity to give love to our Inner Child. Rest allows us to return to our lives replenished, but we must let go of trying to control it to receive what we need. Our Wounded Self may want to put parameters on how much time we take or how deeply we rest, fearing the consequences of our inaction. But without rest, we can do little meaningful work. If we can trust that God's care for us includes meeting our worldly needs, then we can more easily let go of control.

COMMUNICATING WITH GOD

If we are open to it, there is no medium through which God can't communicate. The line in the book we are reading that speaks to a present situation, the friend who calls when we're in need of support but were unwilling to reach out for help, the dream that reveals some inner conflict and inspires us to resolve it, all have significance. Coincidence is only a label we give for such occurrences when we see them without faith. But when we can believe they are for us, then anything in our day-to-day lives can be a vehicle for God's message, offering us the hope, encouragement, or reassurance we need to continue on our journey of recovery.

No length of time needs to separate our communication to God from God's communication to us, as though prayer was delivered via mail and required days or weeks for a reply. When we discover that our relationship with God can be conversational, it becomes more real—*God* becomes more real. It is as if a door, which we had always thought was locked, was, in fact, open, and all that was needed was our willingness to turn the knob. Dialoguing with God is similar to dialoguing with our Inner Child. It is an exchange that happens inside of us—a call and response that arises from deep connection. As with our Inner Child, we give voice to God—we allow God to speak through us… to us. For many, this may sound confusing and even absurd. How we may ask, can we actually embody God's voice? How can we accurately bring the mystery of God into the present moment for us to hear? If anything, it will be our own disbelief in hearing God that prevents us from doing so.

When you can let go of your rational thinking and allow your imagination to guide you, you enter the sacred domain in which God can communicate to you in words. Discerning which are God's words versus your own may take time and practice and may not always be perfectly clear. Yet a good rule of thumb is that God's communication is more likely to come naturally and from your heart, rather than with effort and from your mind. And above all, how you feel after receiving such communication can help you determine its source. If you feel peace, love, and comfort, the communication probably came from God. If you feel stress, fear, or urgency, it probably came from your Wounded Self.

Initially, we may find it useful to dialogue with God in a journal, which may not only help to suspend our disbelief but also record whatever feedback we receive in the exchange. With daily practice, the process becomes more familiar. We pick up a pen and open the door of communication. We may speak with God about matters that are troubling us, for guidance in being a Loving Parent to our Inner Child, or to simply check in about what's going on in our lives. What we hear will be unique to each of us, but can include responses that assuage our fears, affirmations that help us feel supported, or questions asked in response to our own. There is no topic that God won't listen to or offer input on, though it may not always be the message we are expecting or looking for.

Dialoguing with God is not about manipulating a response but coming to God as we are. When we can speak from our hearts—from the deepest parts of ourselves that we feel willing to share—we will receive whatever message we need. Sometimes it doesn't come to us in words, but in a feeling—in the peace and warmth that flows through us after speaking our truth. It is the times when we are most open and vulnerable when we most feel God's presence and love, and isn't this the message we are so often looking for? Such experiences remind us that we are not alone in the work we are doing and that we are cared for every step of the way.

CHAPTER 18

Becoming a Loving Parent to Our Wounded Self

As we strive to become a Loving Parent to our Wounded Child, we will often fall short of our ideals. Some days, we remain connected and in dialogue, feeling our feelings, and on other days we are pulled away in distraction, codependency, and endless doing. Such back and forth can occur on the very same day, hour-to-hour, even moment-to-moment. When our Wounded Child's attachment behavior is activated, and we experience their distress, we'll find that we have two choices: to act from our Wounded Self, which is the habitual route of strategies, or the will of God, which is to choose what's most loving for our Wounded

Child. These wills are *always* in opposition to one another because the will of our Wounded Self is motivated by fear and control, and the will of God is motivated by love and trust.

CHANGING OUR BELIEFS ABOUT OUR WOUNDED SELF

The two powers that influence our will are always present, but which source we listen to is often based on which we listened to previously. Each choice we make influences the next, because the power that we choose gains momentum and energy in our consciousness and has a greater impact on our thinking and behavior. We may have every intention to love our Wounded Child, but unless we are grounded in God's love, we will be unable to follow through with action. Paul the Apostle speaks to this phenomenon:

> *"I do not understand what I do. For what I want to do I do not do, but what I hate I do.... And if I do what I do not want to do... it is no longer I myself who do it, but... sin living in me.... For I have the desire to do what is good, but I cannot carry it out."*[69]
>
> –ROMANS 7:15-19

Despite our sincere desire to making loving choices, we can still be swept away by the power and compulsion of our Wounded Self. The term that Paul uses to refer to our Wounded Self is "sin," and describes the inclination of our Wounded Self as our "sinful nature."[70] As mentioned earlier, though "sin" is associated with religion and has its own particular connotation, the word itself originates from Latin (i.e., "sine") and means "without." From this definition, we can begin to understand the actual nature of our Wounded Self, not as "evil," but merely the reaction of our Inner Child who feels *without* God's love. This was why the Wounded Self manifested before time, and it is why our Wounded Self manifests in our lives today. When we abandon our Wounded Child, we leave them without the love of God, and in this state, our Wounded Self manifests to help them avoid or change the way they feel. It is often *these* Wounded Self strategies that are believed to arise from "sin."

The strategies of our Wounded Self are behaviors that we learned as children and adolescents because they served a purpose. We people-pleased so we could receive love, we controlled our environment so we could feel safe, we engaged in distraction so we could feel less pain. We were simply doing our best with what we had and knew. If we look at the circumstances of our lives, at the abuse and neglect we might have experienced as children, we can see that it was the intelligence of our Wounded Self that helped us to survive. We were not equipped with the ability to be in conscious relationship to our suffering, and so we acted out in various ways to avoid it. What happened, however, is that over time, these coping strategies no longer served us; what began as a way to feel "better" ended up causing more harm than good.

As we come to reflect upon the nature of our Wounded Self, we may only focus on the harm they cause, rather than view their strategies as a misguided attempt to help us feel safe, loved, and without pain. When we act from our Wounded Self, we might call ourselves "bad," just as our parents, society, or religion did. Instead of being shown that we were lovable, despite our behavior, perhaps we were punished in some way—sent to the corner, spanked, or yelled at. Such forms of "discipline" were thought to be enough influence to change our behavior. And so through our experience, which is our greatest teacher, we learned that the part of ourselves that is "bad" or "gets us into trouble" is not worthy of love.

In adulthood, we carry this belief that our behavior reflects our worth—that when we do something "wrong," *we* are "wrong." Yet often, it is no longer the broader society that tells us this, but our internalized society, which looks upon the actions of our Wounded Self with contempt. When we live in disconnection from God's love, we cannot look upon our actions with love, but rather judge ourselves as society has. Instead of viewing our strategies as a reaction to our own self-neglect, we demonize our Wounded Self and call them "evil." Our Wounded Self is a part of us. To hate our Wounded Self is to hate a part of ourselves; to view our Wounded Self as evil is to view a part of us as evil. When we relate to our Wounded Self in this way, it further disconnects us from ourselves; we are not brought to a state of wholeness but are deprived of it.

How we conceptualize our Wounded Self influences the way we relate to them. When we perceive our Wounded Self as a monster, then we relate to them as a monster—as some horrid aspect of ourselves to be locked up and ignored. But just because we ignore our Wounded Self doesn't mean they cease to exist. No matter how well we can be a Loving Parent to our Wounded Child, unless we can bridge the gap that we have made between ourselves and our Wounded Self, we will continue to suffer. We don't want to throw the baby out with the bathwater. Our Wounded Self *is* a part of our Inner Child, but the strategies that they use are not. The more we can separate our Wounded Self's actions from who they are, the better able we can practice love and forgiveness in relationship with them.

• • • • •

Jesus said, "Any house divided against itself will not stand."[71] If we remain divided against ourselves—loving some parts but not others—it is a condition that cannot sustain itself, and certainly one that cannot promote healing and wholeness. The strategies of our Wounded Self are a call for love, not punishment. Like a child, whose acting out is a reflection of their unmet needs, so is the case with our Wounded Self. When we neglect to be a Loving Parent to our Inner Child, we let our Wounded Self live our lives for us, and this is incredibly scary for them because they are just a child. What our Wounded Self needs is love—an unconditional love that says, "I see you, I hear you, and I am here for you." Rather than reprimand them, we seek to understand their behavior and give them what they so desperately desire but are too scared to ask for.

When we walk this path of healing, we are given the opportunity to love as God loves—to love all aspects of ourselves unconditionally. Our Wounded Self is perhaps one of the most misunderstood phenomena in all of humanity. This part of our Inner

Child has been called the "ego," the "devil," and any other term that demoralizes or falsifies its existence. The path to experiencing wholeness does not come from rejecting or "transcending" our Wounded Self, but from loving them. Our Wounded Self is our own fallen angel, cast away not by anything they did but by their own belief in their unworthiness.

Becoming a Loving Parent to our Wounded Self requires changing our beliefs about them. Only when we can perceive our Wounded Self as they really are can we love them for who they are. To love them doesn't mean to condone their behavior, but to practice forgiveness. The actions of our Wounded Self are only the reactions of a child whose needs have not been met and who feels responsible for meeting these needs in the only way they know how. When we can understand our Wounded Self from this perspective, we can begin to cultivate compassion toward them.

No matter what, we must receive the teaching that we are unconditionally loved. This is the truth of who we are, for God loves us unconditionally. Whether we are a "saint" or a "sinner," we are wholly loved by God. The difference between the two is that the saint knows that they are wholly loveable, and the sinner does not; if the sinner knew of their worth in God's eyes, they would experience themselves as whole and without lack. But because they do not know this truth in the depths of their being, their sense of lack makes them seek what is outside of them to feel whole.

How we can most fully know God's love is through embodying it and offering it to our Inner Child. We are asked to become the voice for God that tells our Inner Child of their worth, to become the heart of God that loves our Inner Child unconditionally. To love our Inner Child means to love the whole child—not just parts that are easy to love or those that society approves of, but also those that we have been ashamed of. The parable of *The Prodigal Son* speaks of unconditionally loving our Wounded Self. Jesus tells the story of a son who asked his father for his inheritance and then went out into the world and "wasted his substance with riotous living. And when he had spent all, there arose a mighty famine in that land; and he began to be in want."[72]

Disconnected from the love that bore him, and lost in the wilderness of unconscious living, the son had forgotten who he was and the abundance that was inherently his.

> *And when he came to himself, he said... "I will arise and go to my father, and will say unto him, Father I have sinned against heaven, and before thee. And am no more worthy to be called thy son."*[73]
>
> —LUKE 15:17-18

Much to the son's surprise, however, instead of being punished or rejected for his behavior, he was shown unconditional love. What mattered to the father was not what his son did, but only his return.

Our Wounded Self is the child who goes out into the world and forgets who they are. But we are given the opportunity as a Loving Parent to welcome them back with open arms. It is no small task to change how we relate to our Wounded Self; the messages about this part of ourselves persist throughout society and are maintained by our own self-criticism. Yet when we can recognize that our Wounded Self is *our* Child lost in the dream of scarcity and lack, then we can begin to practice showing them unconditional love. Instead of chastising our Wounded Self for acting in ways that are "bad" or "wrong," we love them back into the knowledge of their True Self. We raise our fallen angel to the heights of their divinity. That is the miracle we are given. When we remind our Wounded Self of who they are, they come to learn that all they sought was already theirs, in full.

TAKING RESPONSIBILITY FOR OUR WOUNDED SELF

We come to experience that there are really three aspects of our Wounded Self, each informed by the strategies of dyadic regulation, autoregulation, and dissociation. While only one aspect may be present at any given time, each can be triggered in reaction to one another. For example, in relationship with our partner, we may engage in codependency, people-pleasing, and approval-seeking (i.e., dyadic regulation strategies) to avoid rejection and abandonment. However, our behavior causes us to abandon our Wounded Child. We may then choose to avoid our partner (i.e., autoregulation strategy) to reconnect with our Wounded Child. Still, our partner's reaction to our avoidance swings us back into dyadic regulation strategies to "save" the relationship. When all of the stress of these dynamics climax, we are most susceptible to engaging in dissociative strategies to numb or change the way we feel.

These internal dynamics can occur anywhere in our lives, from work, to being with family, to everyday decision-making. The common denominator of any Wounded Self reaction is fear—fear of abandonment, fear of insecurity, fear of not having enough, fear of not being good enough, etc. Therefore, learning how to be in relationship with our Wounded Self is learning how to be in relationship with our fears. Though we are powerless over our Wounded Self's reactions, today, we are given more choice in how we respond to them.

The reason we first learn to become a Loving Parent to our Wounded Child—aside from the fact that it is often *their* met or unmet needs that determine the activation of our Wounded Self—is because it is generally easier to be present to our Wounded Child's feelings than to those of our Wounded Self. The energy of our Wounded Self can feel frantic and overwhelming. Their fears are those of a child who feels the responsibility of an adult. Without having had parents who could meet our needs for love and security, our Wounded Self came to believe that our very existence depended on their own volition—which explains the urgency and impulsivity behind so many of our actions. Becoming a Loving Parent to our Wounded Self requires that we change this pattern. Instead of making decisions from our Wounded Self's fear, we learn to come into relationship with it; we give our Wounded Self the space to express how they feel and to tell us what they're afraid of. When we can show up for our Wounded Self in this way their fears diminish and we discover that what they most needed is not control over our environment, but the love and security of a parent.

While previously, we may have felt unable to come into conscious relationship with our Wounded Self, the practice of being a Loving Parent to our Wounded Child makes us more capable. We have developed a greater threshold for emotional discomfort and are more willing to take risks for our recovery. Moreover, our trust in God's care for us gives us the courage to do what feels impossible and reminds us of the truth when the fears of our Wounded Self discount it.

The opportunities we have to be a Loving Parent to our Wounded Self often happen in real-time, when our behavior is being guided by their need for control. We can recognize this state of enmeshment by how we feel. For instance, when we feel stressed or overwhelmed, it is usually an indication that we believe a story our Wounded Self is telling us. Almost any situation in our day-to-day lives can provoke our Wounded Self's fears if we give it the power to influence our sense of security or lovability. Yet rather than look at the story that is motivating our behavior, we become a character in the story and play out the part to lessen our Wounded Self's anxiety. Maybe we're running late to work and are driving recklessly to get there on time, or we've been writing a school paper for hours and hours trying to make it perfect, or we had a conflict with our partner and have since been acquiescing to their every request. Our behavior in each situation is motivated by fear. Fear of being yelled at by our boss or of being fired. Fear of getting a low grade on our paper or of failing our class. Fear that if we don't mend our relationship challenges through overcompensation, our partner will leave us. The stories can be endless, but the core fears of all of them are essentially the same. We're scared of not *having* enough, not *getting* enough, or not *being* enough. When we are living from our Wounded Self, our sense of security and lovability are always on the line; such was often the case when we were young and remains so today without intervention.

• • • • •

Building a conscious relationship with your Wounded Self, so they come to trust in your care for them, happens gradually. Nearly every moment is a decision you can make to either act as your Wounded Self desires and thus reinforce the legitimacy of their fears and need for control or take responsibility for them as a Loving Parent. The first step is noticing when your consciousness is merged with your Wounded Self—when their fear and need for control has become your own. You can observe this in the content of your thoughts and expression of your behavior. While the origin of your Wounded Self's experience arises from fear, the form it takes can be more than its most obvious symptoms. For instance, worry, obsession, regret, guilt, boredom, restlessness, resentment, jealousy, and lust are all states rooted in fear. Pushing these away or ignoring them does little to create peace; entertaining them and getting pulled into their stories is also fruitless. When you can recognize these experiences are ways in which your Wounded Self is trying to communicate with you, then you can turn your attention toward your Wounded Self and give them what they really need.

When you catch yourself acting from your Wounded Self, it creates space between your consciousness and theirs. It is here where you can move out of your enmeshment and into your Loving Parent. Sometimes the awareness of where you are is enough to create that shift; other times, you may need to pause and use whatever tools help you come back into connection with God—into the consciousness of love. From this place, individuated from fear, you can turn toward your Wounded Self and seek to understand their experience. At this juncture, however, you may feel some resistance; the idea of turning toward your Wounded Self—toward fear—can feel like an enigma. Your rational mind may not comprehend what you're being asked to do. And so it's best to just take that faithful step into the unknown. You will find that the moment you actually turn your attention *toward* your Wounded Self, to learn, that all of your confusion leaves you. Your Wounded Self is no longer some insidious force, but a Child—*your* Child—scared, overwhelmed, and in need of love.

The presence of your Wounded Self's thoughts is an indication of having certain unmet needs. Take, for example, worry. When your Wounded Self is worrying about something, they are trying to control an uncertain future to diminish the fear that it provokes. In other words, they are trying to feel a greater sense of security—something they do not presently feel within *you*. While worry happens in your mind, fear is an emotion you can be present to in your body. This is the level where connection and healing occurs. If you were to just brush away your worry, if that were possible, you would miss the opportunity to come into relationship with your Wounded Self and hear their deeper feelings and needs.

When you notice where your mind is, you can step into the consciousness of your Loving Parent and allow your Wounded Self to speak to you about their fears. Similar to dialoguing with your Wounded Child, let the voice and emotion of your Wounded Self find expression, embodying their experience while consciously holding them in love. As you make space for your Wounded Self to be more than just thoughts—more than just "ego stuff"—you'll discover that beneath their worry is a child who is really scared and needing comfort. And so you listen to them. Your intention is not to invalidate or minimize their experience, no matter how irrational their fears may seem, but just to show them through your compassionate attention that you care. If it feels right to acknowledge your Wounded Self's communication in some way, you can, but you don't need to force anything. How you show up for your Wounded Self can often speak more deeply than anything you might say.

Here is a review of the steps you can take to begin responding to your Wounded Self's activation:

1. Notice when your consciousness is merged with your Wounded Self (e.g., you are caught in worry, obsession, regret, guilt, boredom, restlessness, resentment, jealousy, lust—any emotion that causes stress or overwhelm).
2. Reconnect with God, using whatever practices feel right for you (e.g., prayer, meditation, mindful breathing, conscious movement, etc.).
3. Connect with the intention to love your Wounded Self and learn about their experience. If it's helpful, you can bring to

mind an image of yourself as a child (from a photo or your imagination) or place your hands wherever you feel their activation.

4. When you are ready, turn your attention toward your Wounded Self in your body. Notice the sensations and emotions that are present. Allow your Wounded Self's experience to be just as it is, without trying to fix or change it.
5. If it feels right, acknowledge your Wounded Self in some way and make space for them to share with you how they are feeling.
6. Listen and reflect back what you hear. Learn what they need from you. Hold them with compassion. And allow the process to find its natural completion.

As with your Wounded Child, being present to and dialoguing with your Wounded Self can take place solely within yourself, or can include journaling, using props or stuffed animals, or any other medium that works. You have the complete freedom to relate to your Wounded Self in whatever way feels right. When their fear and energy feels too overwhelming, using written dialogue or props can help manage it. If you use a stuffed animal to represent your Wounded Self, you can bring it with you wherever you go, and it can serve as a physical reminder to remain in conscious connection.

• • • • •

Becoming a Loving Parent to our Wounded Self is not a matter of simply telling them that it is time to retire, that their services are no longer needed. They will continue to feel responsible for our lives until we are able to demonstrate our ability to be an adult in the world without their manipulation. Sometimes our Wounded Self's compulsion to act is a misguided attempt to self-soothe, but other times it points to a real need, such as financial stability. When we can first tend to our Wounded Self's distress, we can better discern what, if any, actions are necessary.

Whether it's applying for a new job or planning a weekend getaway, any action can be taken from either our Loving Parent or our Wounded Self. The difference is less about what actions we take than *how* we take them. In our Wounded Self, we fear that whatever can go wrong will go wrong, and so try to manipulate circumstances to create the outcome we want, but in our Loving Parent, we take action grounded in faith. We still have to take the steps that any action requires, but our trust in God's care for us lessens our attachment to the results. This helps us to remain in connection with our Inner Child instead of abandoning them through our use of strategies.

Our goal as a Loving Parent is to learn how to incorporate our Wounded Self into our day-to-day lives. A way we can do this is by taking action *with* our Wounded Self instead of in separation from them. We let them be our passenger while we steer the ship. They may still jockey for position if the stakes feel high, but if during such times we can pause, be present to their activation, and return to our intention for connectedness, it can help them feel included without having to take control.

It is our trust in God's care for us that engenders our Wounded Self's trust in our care for them. When we take action as a Loving Parent and experience results that meet our needs, it gives our Wounded Self evidence that we are capable of being an adult—that they no longer have to do that for us. Yet, it is a process that happens over time. We may find it easier to act from our Loving Parent in some areas of our lives than others. Perhaps we're emotionally vulnerable with our partner but still engage in perfectionism at work, or we practice mindful eating but continue to impulsively clean our home. What's most important is that we remain willing to learn where we still struggle to surrender our need for control and continue taking risks to do so.

Being in relationship with our Wounded Self heals their trauma of having to live as an adult. Every time we revoked that responsibility, we gave it to them, and they, in turn, had to navigate our life circumstances alone. But when we can show our Wounded Self that we are capable of being a Loving Parent, both in how we show up for them and in how we take action in the world, we give them permission to be a child again.

• • • • •

We can learn to develop healthy relationships with many activities that were once motivated by our Wounded Self by changing *how* we engage in them. However, there may be some that we must abstain from to continue growing in our recovery. If we have a history of addiction to mind- and mood-altering substances, for instance, using them again will only activate the same patterns of behavior and send us back down the road of involuntary dependence. This can be the case with any addiction from our past, such as gambling or our use of pornography. The more deeply rooted the behavior, the more power it has over our ability to practice moderation or restraint. After some time of abstinence, we may think partaking in such activities might work out okay, but doing so will only result in the same insanity and unmanageability that we experienced in our lives before—or worse.

Sometimes being a Loving Parent to our Wounded Self requires us to say "*no*" to what they desire, especially if the consequences of acting on such desires put our recovery at risk. Our temptation to return to old, self-destructive behaviors is the result of not having yet found the rhythm of self-care that meets our needs. Until we can trust in the peace and security that come from relationship with our Inner Child and with God, our Wounded Self will continue to desire using strategies that, for a time, "worked." On such occasions, we're prone to recall only the pleasures of our using rather than the bottoms it took us to, and if we entertain these stories for too long, we make ourselves vulnerable to relapse.

The gift of our recovery is fragile, and one that we must protect, for no amount of it can guarantee lasting freedom from the dysfunction and unmanageability that once ruled our lives. Creating boundaries and learning to uphold them is part of being a Loving Parent to our Wounded Self. It is our way of honoring the sacred container we have built in relationship with our Inner Child. What these boundaries look like may vary depending upon the situation. Still, they all concern our ability to say "*no*" to behaviors or activities that threaten our new way of life, not just those that seek false comforts, but those that resist the discomfort of our healing. Our Wounded Self is in the decisions we make to cut our morning meditation short, to put off dialoguing with our Wounded Child, to go only halfway into feeling our pain.... We must also learn to say "*no*" to these compulsions that arise from complacency, for they too undermine our recovery.

Saying "*no*" to our Wounded Self does not mean shutting them out or closing the door on connection. It is merely the first step we take to communicate clear boundaries and reaffirm our commitment to our recovery. The next step is to make space for our Wounded Self to tell us what they are feeling and needing. When we connect with them in this way, the compulsion to act from our Wounded Self will leave us, for meeting our Inner Child's deeper need for love releases our Wounded Self's attachment to strategies. While we may have to return to this practice, again and again, it offers us the opportunity to come into relationship with our Wounded Self, and it is *relationship* that builds the foundation for our recovery.

FORGIVING OUR WOUNDED SELF

The motivation of our Wounded Self to act in a particular way is to feel better. That's all. If we as a Loving Parent are absent, then the decision to act as our Wounded Self desires will be made for us. But if we can be present to our Wounded Self's experience, we will find that such desires naturally diminish. Where, at first, we felt caught in the undertow of their temptation, now we have passed through the urge and are resting above the water. Yet showing up for our Wounded Self in this way is not easy, especially on days when we feel tired, stressed, or burnt out. When our gas tank for self-care is low, we are more susceptible to using strategies to avoid how we feel. We may tell ourselves that because we've had a hard week, finished our to-do list, or performed well at work that we deserve a reward.... Any one of these explanations is worthy of treating ourselves kindly. But we have to discern, especially when we're feeling emotionally drained and spiritually disconnected, whether our choices are truly loving. Will they help our Inner Child feel seen and heard, or support our conscious contact with God? Allowing ourselves space and time to really feel into these answers can help us know the truth.

Reorienting the way we live takes time and commitment. Before, we may have gone about our day without considering our motivation for doing something. Our Wounded Self called the shots, and we acted accordingly. We were unaware of how seemingly harmless activities, such as using social media or browsing the Internet, affected our Inner Child. Yet as we have become more conscious, we are more sensitive to experiencing the emotional and spiritual consequences of our actions. While this helps us to remain in touch with how we are living, it also makes us more vulnerable to self-judgment.

When we act from our Wounded Self and get the same results, we can feel guilty or ashamed—that we "should have known better." But the irony is that when we make the unloving choice to engage in a strategy, we can make the additionally unloving choice to self-loathe for having done so. We reprimand our Wounded Self, just as a parent might do with their child, in the belief that shaming them will change their behavior. However, when we reject our Wounded Self, it only provokes their use of more strategies to avoid or change the way they feel. Conditional love does little to create the outcome we want; it only perpetuates the guilt and shame we're trying to avoid.

In our recovery, we try to be "perfect" and forget that we are also still human, subject to acting from our Wounded Self. Part of our healing is learning how to practice self-forgiveness in response to the choices we make. In *A Course in Miracles,* it is said, "You will not find peace until you have removed the nails from the hands of God's Son, and taken the last thorn from his forehead."[74] When we act from our Wounded Self and hate ourselves for having done so, we are attacking our own Inner Child—the Child of God—who was given to us to love unconditionally. Our hatred toward ourselves reinforces our Child's belief of being unlovable and keeps them in exile. To heal, we must take the "Son of God" down from the cross and remove the thorns from their forehead; we must practice self-forgiveness instead of self-condemnation.

The purpose of the human condition is not so we can *become* perfect, but so we can learn to love ourselves in our imperfection. In such love—in the unblemished recognition of who we are, regardless of what we do or don't do—we realize that we already *are* perfect. That is the meaning of *The Prodigal Son*. Beneath the outward dysfunction of our Wounded Self's behavior is the desperation and aloneness they feel, as well as the messages they tell themselves about what they need to be okay. Understanding what motivates our Wounded Self to act as they do helps us to have compassion for them instead of resentment. We come to recognize their behavior as a call for love, and when we can offer them love through our practice of forgiveness, we teach our Wounded Self of their worth and lovability.

CHAPTER 19

Becoming a Loving Parent to Our Core Child

The deepest layer of our Inner Child is our Core Child—this is the essence of who we are. The characteristics of our Core Child are an innate sense of wonder, curiosity, joy, playfulness, openness, and compassion. The personal characteristics of our Core Child are how these qualities manifest in our lives. Without wounding and conditioning, we would all be the divine expression of our authentic selves. Humanity would look very different. Yet the reality is that society has impacted us in ways that diminish our Core Child's presence. The abuse we have experienced, the false messages that we have taken as truth, the cultural influence that has misguided us, have all led us away from knowing and *being* who we really are.

In the Strange Situation Procedure,[75] it was shown that children with secure attachment styles engaged in play and exploration naturally. Their trust in their parent's care for them allowed them to be themselves. However, those with insecure attachment styles, whose parents did not adequately meet their needs, could not as easily engage in play; their worry and distress prevented them from feeling safe enough to do so. Such is what occurred for many of us growing up. Without the love, support, and encouragement we needed to thrive, we became a shadow of our authentic selves.

The fall from embodying our Core Child was a gradual process, which occurred in relationships with our families and society. When we experienced rejection in response to our authentic expression, we were given messages that had long-lasting impact. For instance, if, as a kid, we loved to dance and were told by our dance instructor that we weren't any good, then that message may have thwarted our very love for dancing. We loved it because it allowed us to express ourselves through movement; it was not about being anything other than who we were. But the messages we may have been given made dance into something else—not play, but comparison and competition. If we didn't drop dancing altogether, we might have gone forward from our Wounded Self, no longer dancing for joy and expression but for meeting the expectations of others, for approval seeking, and for being good enough. Such a scenario may have occurred in any area of interest, such as music, theatre, visual arts, sports, reading, or learning. An unloving message may have been enough to turn us away from what we loved forever.

In addition to the discouraging messages we may have received from others, the cultural influence of society had its own impact. "Growing up" and becoming adults often meant letting go of our Core Child's desires, not just the particular things we loved to do, but why we loved them. Activities of play gave us moments of reprieve from the responsibilities and expectations of life. They were sacred space from which the "shoulds" and "have-to's" didn't enter. Yet as we transitioned from childhood to adolescence to adulthood, we were told we had to turn our attention away from "childish things" and onto more pragmatic goals. This is not to say we let go of our joys and passions completely, but our natural instinct to live from this place diminished. *Being* was replaced by *doing*. Living in the freedom of what *is* was replaced by seeking to *become* and acquire what is not yet ours.

FOSTERING A RELATIONSHIP WITH OUR CORE CHILD

While our Core Child may feel lost to us, they are not. They are only waiting for us to create space for them to exist. When we learn to be a Loving Parent whom our Inner Child can trust and depend on, we help them feel safe enough to play again. Our experience of this often comes naturally, during moments when we feel the weight of our lives lift from our shoulders. We are brought into the present moment, when we laugh from our bellies in joy and contentment, or when the warmth of being loved by our own love opens our hearts. The presence of our Core Child brings us back to living from our authentic selves. Yet it also makes us feel like a child again—our sense of wonder, curiosity, and playfulness manifest in everyday activities, as we spend time in nature, take up a new hobby, or let go of our inhibitions and express ourselves.

Our Core Child has their own consciousness and with that their own particular needs. Dialoguing with them is a great way to learn about what those needs are and how we as a Loving Parent can meet them. Even if we're not used to talking to our Core Child because they are a part of our Inner Child, we have some familiarity with what it means to communicate with them. However, we'll find it easiest to do so when the needs of our Wounded Child and Wounded Self have first been met. When the outer layers of our Inner Child are at peace, it allows us to be present to what's underneath.

Our intention when dialoguing with our Core Child is to learn how to support their needs for expression, playfulness, and joy. Sometimes they may tell us right away what they desire. Other times, if it feels difficult to receive a clear response, we can ask them what they enjoyed doing when we were young. It may have been reading fiction, being in nature, painting, dancing, singing, spending time with friends, or going on adventures. Whatever lights us up is a good indication that our Core Child feels excited about it.

After learning what our Core Child desires, we can take action as a Loving Parent. Maybe they want to make artwork again or read a fun book before bedtime. These desires might be quite easy to integrate into our daily lives: we go out and get some art materials or sign up for an art class, or we go to a bookstore and pick out a book that feels exciting to read. Other desires, however, might provoke some resistance. When the needs of our Inner Child feel in conflict with one another, it is more often the result of trauma, which creates blocks in pursuing what our Core Child desires, rather than some inherent aversion to it. When we take steps in meeting each of our Inner Child's needs, we don't have to compromise. Say, for example, that our Core Child wants to attend a social event because it sounds fun. The idea of being around a lot of people, however, activates the trauma of our Wounded Child, who associates such contexts with being bullied or rejected. Our Wounded Self, therefore, will want to avoid the social event to protect our Wounded Child and feel safe.

When deciding whether or not to go to the social event, our initial instinct may be to listen to our Wounded Self, whose need to protect our Wounded Child overrides our Core Child's need for play and connection with others. Yet if we slow down our process, we'll find that there is a way to meet all of our Inner Child's needs. The first step we can take as a Loving Parent is to acknowledge our Wounded Child's feelings. They may tell us how going to the event reminds them of being at school, when they were picked on and had no one to protect them. Their fear of being around a lot of people is that it will result in experiencing the same type of rejection. As we listen, we connect with our Wounded Child in their memories and validate their experience; we show up for them in a way that they didn't receive in their past, and by doing so, meet their needs for grieving and comfort.

The next step we take is to learn how to support our Wounded Self. Their need to protect our Wounded Child is the result of not having had protection when we were young, and so their strategy to avoid the event is a way to prevent retraumatization. Though we can't predict the outcome of attending the event, we can reassure our Wounded Self that if we were to experience some form of rejection we would respond to it in a way that helps them feel safe. We as a Loving Parent become the protector that our Wounded Child never had and thus help our Wounded Self let go of that responsibility. When both our Wounded Child and Wounded Self trust us to care for them, it allows us to take the action that would meet our Core Child's needs for play and connection with others.

Here are steps you can take when the needs of your Inner Child are in conflict and prevent you from supporting your Core Child's desires:

1. When you feel inspired to engage in an activity with your Core Child but also experience inner conflict of some kind (which can be felt as overwhelm, confusion, or unease), take a moment to pause and breathe.
2. Reconnect with God, using whatever practices feel right for you (e.g., prayer, meditation, mindful breathing, conscious movement, etc.).
3. Connect with the intention to love all parts of your Inner Child and learn about their experience.
4. When you are ready, first turn your attention toward your Wounded Child in your body. Notice the sensations

wherever you feel them and the emotion that is present. Allow their experience to be just as it is, without trying to fix or change it. Acknowledge them and make space for them to share with you how they are feeling. Listen, and learn about what they need from you to feel safe and loved.

5. Next, turn your attention toward your Wounded Self. Allow their experience to be just as it is, without trying to fix or change it. Acknowledge them and make space for them to share with you how they are feeling, what their fears are, and what they need from you to let go of control.
6. Check to see if there is any remaining tension or conflict in your body. If there is, try to stay present, feel, and learn about what is unresolved. If you feel peace, calm, or a sense of relief, you can then check in with your Core Child and confirm their desire to engage in the particular activity.
7. Finally, make a commitment to follow through with what your Core Child desires and take action.

It may take a while for us to heal the trauma that has kept us from doing what we love, but we don't need to wait until we are healed to do them—we just need to show up for whatever parts of us are activated and walk through the steps that bring us back into alignment. While it may at times feel like a lot of work, the result is that we create an environment within ourselves that allows us to experience the joy of what we're doing.

THE GIFTS OF RELATIONSHIP

Part of what is so special about doing things with our Core Child is that we're doing them together. Whether it is reading a book, walking in nature, or drawing a picture, we allow the activity to be a time for connection and remain open to whatever communication our Core Child may have. For instance, if we are reading a book, we can pause and ask our Core Child how they feel about what is happening. Offering them this invitation is like opening a door to a magical world. The book becomes a richer, more exciting experience than we may have ever had reading alone.

Being with our Core Child takes us to that timeless place of play and exploration; it becomes its own joyous activity. We begin to see the world as our Core Child sees it—full of wonder—and feel our relationship to the world as they feel it—at one with the birds and trees. It's as if we were alive for the first time, awake to the inherent beauty within all things. We'll find that our Core Child's need for "play" doesn't always have to mean joyous, but genuine and uninhibited. When we can show up to life with the willingness to be present to whatever is in us and with the courage to allow for its expression, then we can always return again and again to the natural state of who we are.

A gift of being in relationship with our Core Child is that we are more open to what excites us, what inspires us, and what we feel called to manifest in the world. Where before we felt alone in what we made of our life, now we are better able to listen to what we desire and follow our hearts. Yet even what our Core Child inspires can become a strategy of our Wounded Self. The steps we take to make our dreams a reality become a way to feel more worthy of our gifts; the attainment of our goals become a way to feel more deserving of love—the love of our parents, of society, and more important but often overlooked, the love of God. We project our childhood experience of conditional love onto God and believe that God will only love us if we meet our "God-given potential."

On an intellectual level, we may believe in God's unconditional love, but it doesn't sink in until our Inner Child feels it. This is where our Loving Parent comes in. When we pursue a passion and experience the activation of our Wounded Self, rather than continue acting from their motivation, we take time to listen to their fears and reassure them of their lovability. The love we give them sinks down into the messages we received as children, that said only when we do something worthy of love are we given it, and heals these false beliefs. As a result, our relationship with what we feel passionate about and inspired to create changes. With trust in God's care for us, expressing our gifts becomes a shared journey—one we take with our Inner Child and God. We may not know where it will lead us, but the outcome is sure to be more fulfilling than any we could have devised on our own.

CHAPTER 20

Supporting the Expression of Our Authentic Self

In our childhood and adolescence, we were taught that expressing our authentic self would result in rejection. We craved belonging because rejection is what we most feared. Even after taking considerable steps toward being a Loving Parent to our Inner Child, the temptation to belong within a culture can overpower our need to be who we are. We fear that challenging the norms of society—those that our family adopted and which influenced our belief systems and patterns of behavior—will result in the same rejection we experienced when we were young.

The tragedy is that society doesn't create a safe, unconditionally loving environment that supports the expression of our authentic self. If society held this as sacred, then crying in public would be as welcome as laughter. Praying in public would be as common as checking our phones. If all forms of expression were permissible, there would be much less trauma, mental illness, violence, and suicide. Where there is love and acceptance, there is healing.

An important teaching of Jesus was to honor the expression of our authentic self:

> *His followers said, "When will you appear to us and when shall we see you?" Jesus said, "When you strip without being ashamed and you take your clothes and put them under your feet like little children and trample them, then* [you] *will see the child of the living one and you will not be afraid."*[76]
>
> –THE GOSPEL OF THOMAS, 37

At that time in history, society was bound by repression, rigidity, and control. Jesus was perceived as a threat because his teachings challenged society's norms, which helped people feel safe from doing "wrong" and experiencing rejection. However, it was these norms propagated by religious law that restricted people's experience of the truth: that who they were, no matter their life choices, was wholly worthy of God's love. Only in the freedom of expressing who we are can we experience our inherent lovability, for it is in this place of vulnerability that we feel the closest to God.

There is little difference between then and now. The collective culture upholds particular norms that restrict the expression of our authentic self. Society tells us how to think, speak, look, feel, and behave to remain within the confines of its approval. To be different can result in being ridiculed, pathologized, or ostracized. Moreover, the trauma of being rejected for expressing our authentic self is carried with us, so that even if the culture around us changes, we can still believe that the consequences for being ourselves remain the same. To avoid rejection, we clothe ourselves with the messages of society; we conform our behavior, stifle our truths, constrict our movement, and silence our voices. When we sacrifice our authenticity for society's approval, we lose touch with the Child in us. "Where art thou?"[77] asked God when Adam and Eve clothed themselves and hid in fear of rejection. Who are we when we clothe ourselves in society's garments?

FREEING OURSELVES FROM THE NORMS

Jesus's encouragement to "strip without being ashamed"[78] is a revelatory act—one that asks us to remove the masks and armor that have kept us "safe," but which has limited our experience of freedom. Until we make this decision to be who we are, no matter where we are, we will be enslaved by society's norms. Being our authentic self in the world is only scary when we believe that society holds power to judge us. The greatest injuries are not the words or actions of others, but the false messages given by them that tell us we are worthy of rejection. However, this path of recovery allows us to awaken to the truth of who we are. Through unconditionally loving our Inner Child, we give ourselves a message that speaks louder than the lies we received. God wants us to live our lives naked—uninhibited—for only then can we experience the Garden of Eden. While it is a state of vulnerability, it is also one of fearlessness. We are choosing to live from our authentic self because we know we are protected—not by strategies, but by God's love.

It takes courage to express ourselves in public; we fear that to be sad, anxious, depressed, angry, or even joyful may cause others to feel uncomfortable. Yet their reaction is not because we are doing something "wrong," but because such expression is not openly practiced in society. When the unspoken norm is to inhibit our authentic expression, it can feel scary to honor our experience as it is. We make ourselves visible when we embody what yearns for expression, and to be visible is to be vulnerable to the judgment of others. Our trauma of having been rejected for being ourselves is activated in these moments. Our Wounded Self fears that if we choose to express ourselves, we'll experience the same results. It is a valid concern, yet our trauma, which harkens back to past experience, does not often speak to present reality. Unless we can respond to these fears from our Loving Parent, we will be unable to free ourselves from our conditioned behavior.

We may find that it is not only expressing emotion or turning toward our Inner Child in public that we feel resistance to, but also seeking connection with God. Choosing to pray or meditate around others, or act in any way that is indicative of spiritual practice, can feel just as terrifying as anything else. Our Wounded Self may fear that our behavior will be judged as "weakness" or that it will provoke reactions from those who resent religion and make us the target of their misdirected anger. Whatever our fears are, if we feel resistance from our Wounded Self, we can turn toward them and be present to their experience. We want to reassure them that no matter how others react, we will be there for them as a Loving Parent.

In *A Course in Miracles*, it is said, "Defenselessness is strength. It testifies to recognition of the Christ in you."[79] At any moment, when we are not protecting against the fear of rejection but choosing to express what is in our hearts, we are reaffirming that our worth and value are not given to us by others but by God. In giving ourselves permission to express our truth, we experience our divinity.

CHAPTER 21

Living from Integration

Integration occurs after we have come into relationship with each aspect of our Inner Child. We learn that we are made up of many parts, but that all originate from our oneness with God. When we are at peace, we are in touch with this reality; when we are in distress, we are out of touch with this reality. And yet coming back to the truth of who we are occurs from simply turning to what is present in us with unconditional love. As human beings, we will invariably move in and out of connection with our Inner Child—it is a part of the process of learning what disconnects us and what reconnects us. But gradually we learn how to stay together for longer and how to return more quickly after having left.

Each aspect of our Inner Child can feel like a distinct personality, and yet each is a part of the whole. Though it takes consistent practice to be present to the diversity of our Inner Child's experience, our love for them helps us find the willingness to do so.

Relationship with our Inner Child grows our ability to love, and it is love that transforms our relationship with them. It is akin to the alchemical process of turning lead into gold, but this transmutation is not the result of changing the substance, but rather our love for it. What we once saw as lead has *always* been gold; only in relating to it from love can we see it for what it really is.

When we are in conscious contact with God, our ability to be present to whatever arises in us is possible. Even if we notice resistance to feeling our feelings, which is an indication that we are in our Wounded Self, our connection with God allows for us to turn toward our Wounded Self's resistance and start there. Though it may feel easier to bypass the resistance to access the feelings underneath, it is often most helpful to start with whatever is at the surface. Any experience is an important experience and one that asks for us to turn to it with love. When we acknowledge our Wounded Self's fear of feeling what is present, then it can more easily give way to the feelings beneath the fear. Guided by love, we move from one experience to the next, and our whole Child feels seen and heard.

Wherever we are, whatever we are doing, we carry the intention to be with all parts of our Inner Child. This gives permission for any communication or emotion to arise in us instead of being blocked by our resistance to feeling it. For instance, when reading with our Core Child, it is possible that at some point, the storyline activates old wounds. Perhaps the main character loses a parental figure, and our Wounded Child's association with this event immediately gives rise to grief. Rather than push aside these emotions to continue reading, we can stay with our Wounded Child. Though the inspiration to read came from our Core Child, our Wounded Child is also present and may have something important they want to share. Reading with our Core Child, therefore, becomes a serendipitous opportunity for healing.

• • • • •

In *Jesus the Son of Man*, Kahlil Gibran speaks of Jesus as the epitome of integration: "His body was single, and each part seemed to love every other part."[80] When we become a Loving Parent to our Inner Child, we are both single *and* made of parts. Our rootedness in God enables us to be in relationship with each part so that love is the thread that binds our whole being as one. We no longer relate to our Inner Child as though they were separate from us or as though one aspect of our Inner Child were separate from another. Love brings unity and integration to what was once a state of disunity and disintegration. When we enter a state of integration, the connectedness our Inner Child feels with us is the same connectedness that we feel with God. God is the source of our comfort, and our presence to our Inner Child is their comfort. And it is also God's comfort that is their comfort. In relationship to our Inner Child, we embody God's love, and we *are* God's love; in that love, our Inner Child doesn't feel abandoned by us, and we don't feel without God.

At the most basic level of miracles, Jesus was a human being, like us, and was given the same conditions from which to overcome and to heal. When we can view him in this way—as someone who learned to become a Loving Parent to their Inner Child—then we can more easily believe that what was possible for Jesus is also possible for us. We all have our own history of trauma, conditioning, and struggle and yet we all share the same building blocks, and therefore the same potential for recovery. The gift is given to all of us, regardless of our differences. We all have an Inner Child, and we are all unconditionally loved by God. The question is whether we choose to take this journey and be open to the miracles that come.

CHAPTER 22

Experiencing God's Love

When the Wounded Self created the universe, they were willing to let go of the truth of who they were to avoid the pain of abandonment. The Wounded Self's rejection of their wound was unknowingly their own rejection of themselves. As the Child, they only wished to experience God's love, but to experience it, they had to be removed from it—a concept discussed in *Conversations with God.*[81] Born in perfect love, in the oneness of God, the Child could not experience their own reality. We can, therefore, understand our embodiment as human beings as a necessary catalyst for experiencing God's love.

The parable of the *Prodigal Son,* referred to in Chapter 18, also speaks to this very idea. When the younger son returned home after many years of being away, the father was joyous and made arrangements to celebrate. However, the elder son, who had remained with his father, was angry and jealous. He could not understand why he, despite his loyalty, had never received such a celebration. And the father said to him:

> *"My son... you are always with me, and everything I have is yours. But we had to celebrate and be glad because this brother of yours was dead and is alive again; he was lost and is found."*[82]
>
> –LUKE 15:31-32

The two sons in this parable represent our two realities: that of being eternally one with God, as it was in the beginning before time, and that of being embodied in the physical universe. Both realities exist, and neither is without God's presence and love. Yet the difference is that in the absolute reality, our awareness of God's love is without contrast, and therefore without the means to experience it. This is the condition of the elder son. Though his father says that he is ever with him and that all he has is his, the elder son never felt the kind of love that was given to his younger brother; it was because this brother was dead and alive again, lost and then found that he could actually experience it.

"You don't know what you've got till it's gone" is a contemporary saying that reflects an ancient truth. In the Garden of Eden, God forbids Adam and Eve from eating of the Tree of Knowledge of Good and Evil, saying that doing so will result in their death. When Eve mentions this to the serpent, it says, "You are not going to die, but God knows that as soon as you eat of it your eyes will be opened and you will be like divine beings who know good and bad."[83] Without having metaphorically eaten from the Tree of Knowledge of Good and Evil, we could not have created the conditions necessary to experience God's love.

OVERCOMING SEPARATION

Our embodiment as human beings and the trauma we experienced with our parents and society can be compared to eating from the Tree of Knowledge of Good and Evil. Though we didn't choose to experience such painful circumstances, they created the feeling of being separate from unconditional love. Living from our trauma, engaging in strategies, and oblivious to our Inner Child, we were banished from the Garden of Eden. We wandered helplessly, seeking a way to return, but not knowing how. Just as God placed the Tree of Knowledge of Good and Evil and the Tree of Life at the center of the Garden of Eden, so God places our Inner Child at the center of our consciousness. In our Inner Child's wounding, we experience the "fall," but in our reunion with them, we experience the Tree of Life.

In *A Course in Miracles*, it is said:

> *Healing is accomplished the instant the sufferer no longer sees any value in pain. Who would choose suffering unless he thought it brought him something, and something of value to him?*[84]

If we experience suffering because we desire it, our desire for it is because it creates contrast to what we *really* desire—the feeling of unconditional love. We are the authors of our experience, and we would not choose suffering unless we thought it somehow benefited us. The impulse to experience unconditional love is misguided by our Wounded Self, but as we become a Loving Parent to our Inner Child, that feeling manifests. When our Wounded Self recognizes the love they seek can be found in us, we no longer need to create separation to feel unconditional love.

• • • • •

> [Jesus] *called a little child to him, and placed the child among* [his disciples]. *And he said: "Truly I tell you, unless you change and become like little children, you will never enter the Kingdom of Heaven."*[85]
>
> –MATTHEW 18:3

It may be said that Jesus's comment describes the way in which we can experience God's love. Within our consciousness, we are both our Loving Parent *and* our Inner Child. As a Loving Parent, it is God's love that we give to our Inner Child, and God's love that we receive *as* our Inner Child. We are both the giver and receiver—both God and God's Child. In that sense, being a Loving Parent to our Inner Child allows us to "become as little children" so that by receiving God's love, we enter "the Kingdom of Heaven."

The doorway to experiencing our divinity is in relationship with our Inner Child, for it is this that allows us to experience the aspect of God that loves unconditionally and the aspect of God that is the experience of unconditional love. When we have entered into this place where the belief in separation is healed, we realize our oneness with God. Yet we are not asked to become perfect to maintain this realization. The beauty of life is the meeting of our humanity and our divinity, where the circumstances of our lives become opportunities to practice unconditional love. For instance, as a Loving Parent to our Wounded Child, we experience God's love as understanding and compassion; to our Wounded Self, we experience it as acceptance and forgiveness; and to our Core Child, we experience it as the complete permission to be ourselves. No matter the circumstance, we are given the opportunity to be conduits of God's Love, for only through us can God's Child know God's love experientially.

In relationship with our Inner Child and God, there is a continuous opening to God's love. Our relationship with God allows us to be a Loving Parent to our Inner Child. As we give love to our Inner Child, it helps them feel secure in our care for them, and in their security, we feel a greater sense of openness. We move from being closed and disconnected to being open and connected, and in this state, we are better able to receive God's love. The more open our connection with God, the deeper our connection with our Inner Child, and so on. A way to show this process might look like this:

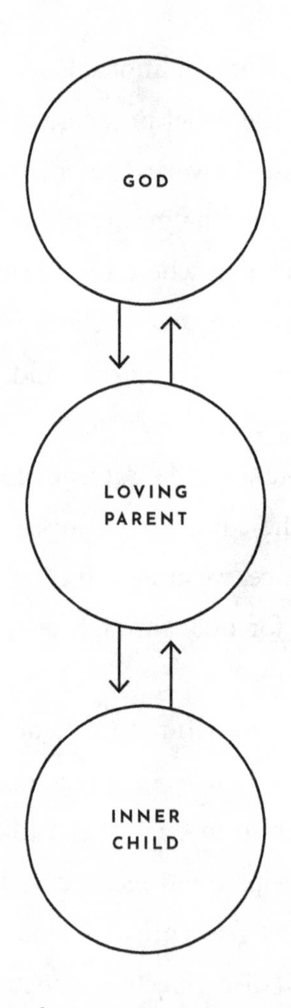

In this diagram, God, our Loving Parent, and our Inner Child are in a continuous giving and receiving of love. However, as a Loving Parent, we are responsible for actively attending to both our own need for conscious contact with God and our Inner Child's need for conscious contact with us. *We* are the variable that keeps this process running; it is we who turn to God, and we who turn to our Inner Child. The channels of giving and receiving are inherently a part of us, and though it requires our conscious effort to keep the flow going, over time and with consistency, we become a part of the flow.

Being in the flow of continuous giving and receiving—from God to us, from us to our Inner Child, from our Inner Child to us, and from us to God—is what Jesus may have been referring to when he said, "Truly, truly, I say to you, you will see heaven opened, and the angels of God ascending and descending on the Son of Man."[86] It is our humanity—our being the "Son of Man"—that offers us the experience of God's love so that by such love, we come to know ourselves as the "Son of God."

PART IV

Relationship with Others

Teach only love, for that is what you are.[87]

–IN A COURSE IN MIRACLES

CHAPTER 23

Loving Others

Cultivating a relationship with our Inner Child and God offers rewards that extend well beyond our personal lives. Before recovery, we may have often engaged in relationships with others from our Wounded Self, unconsciously driven by strategies to feel loved, accepted, and to avoid the pain of rejection. We made people our gods, beginning with our parents, and then our friends, partners, teachers, employers, and society at large. Without recognition of our own worth, we looked to the world to tell us who we were. Yet this dependence upon the world prevented us from experiencing our wholeness, which does not come from outside of us but inside.

In relationship to our Inner Child, we learn that what we sought from others was the message that we were good enough, lovable enough, or special enough. We were looking for the parent that we always wanted but never had—one who could love us unconditionally. The gift of recovery is that *we* get to become that parent who can love our Inner Child in the way they always needed. We are no longer driven by the false belief that others' perception is an indication of who we are. Without our dependence upon others for our sense of self-worth, we can more easily be in relationship with them.

Our Wounded Self clings to relationships in the belief they can offer us a sense of wholeness, yet it is precisely our attachment to relationships that prevents us from feeling it. Jesus said:

> *"Everyone who has left houses or brothers or sisters or father or mother or wife or children or fields for my sake will receive a hundred times as much and will inherit eternal life."*[88]
>
> –MATTHEW 19:29

To "leave" our relationships is not about rejecting them but moving away from the notion that they can offer us what is inherently ours. When we make loving our Inner Child most important, our relationships naturally improve, because we are not entering them from a place of lack but wholeness. From this place, we can really *be* in relationship with others. It becomes a sharing of love rather than a taking of love, and in this way, we are given a hundred times as much than what we sought beforehand.

When our needs for self-love are met, we can give and receive love without conditions. Our giving is without expectation of getting anything in return, for when we are full, giving is the natural flow. Yet, in this state, we are also more open to receiving love from others without attachment to how it is given. We no longer perceive such love as a need left unfulfilled but as a gift that meets the love within us, already manifest. This sharing of love becomes water flowing into water. Nothing is lost, only gained.

PUTTING OURSELVES FIRST

Our Wounded Self may fear what will happen to our relationships if we put loving ourselves first—that we'll be rejected or abandoned. We have to be willing to let go of our attachment to relationships to truly honor our needs, and this means accepting others' reactions to our choices. Society has supported the value of putting others' needs before our own—that it is righteous—but it is this self-sacrifice that often leads to codependency, resentment, and violence. Our Wounded Self's fear of rejection and abandonment for putting our needs before others is likely because we have had these experiences throughout our lives. When we have relationships with people who don't love themselves first, they place expectations on us to meet these needs for them. When not met, they in their Wounded Self reject or abandon us. Neglecting our needs will always result in living from our Wounded Self and therefore living from strategies and reactions. We can cosign each other's codependency, but it will not lead to a sharing of love, but a taking of love. We only have so much to give when our wells are solely filled by one another.

Gradually we learn how to remain in relationship with our Inner Child while in relationship with others. To the best of our ability, we tend to our Inner Child's needs as they arise and are gentle with ourselves in the process. We may find it helpful to discuss with those whom we are in relationship with what we are doing, for how we live and what choices we make may look different than for many. Being in conscious relationship with ourselves while in relationship with others is not the norm for society; we aren't raised or taught to live in this manner. While we may choose to do so, others may not. Being open, vulnerable, and honest—traits that have blossomed for us in our recovery—may feel uncomfortable and scary for others, just as it once was for us. We cannot force anyone to meet us here. We all have our own path and make our own decisions, and one of the most difficult things is learning to accept this reality—that what we hoped our relationships could be may not be so, at least for now. Part of this practice is learning how to love others where they are, and sometimes we need to grieve the loss of what we wanted before we can move into acceptance.

• • • • •

Being in relationship with others is a mirror that shows us how we love ourselves. The commandment, "Thou shalt love thy neighbor as thyself," doesn't speak of the kind of love to give to one another. This is rather a statement of truth—that we are given the ability to love others as much as we love ourselves. If we take time every day to be present to our Inner Child, feel what we are feeling, and rest in the quiet comfort of God, we are better able to love and be present to others. When our Inner Child's needs are met, we can enter into relationship without expectation. Yet when we neglect to meet their needs, our Wounded Self becomes activated, and we forget that it's not others' responsibility to make us happy, nor others' fault when we are not.

"Thou shalt withhold love from thy neighbor as thy withhold love from thyself," though not a commandment, is just as true as its opposite. When we withhold love from ourselves, we are unable to give from the spiritual well within us. Deepening our relationship with the interiority of our life, where God and our Inner Child reside, is the process by which our spiritual well is filled. It is a well filled over time, yet also one we must fill each and every day. As we learn to be a Loving Parent to our Inner Child, we build within us a foundation for love, which enables us to give unto others as we give unto ourselves.

Loving others unconditionally was the teaching that Jesus demonstrated in his life. Sharing the same human condition, we can assume that his ability to love all kinds of people was a result of loving all parts of himself. Our judgment toward others is often a projection of our own self-judgment. When we can love all parts of ourselves, we no longer project these parts onto others and reject them for what they reflect back in us. Our ability to love others comes from having loved ourselves first. When we experience God's love in the depth of our being, it brings down the walls of separation and allows us to commune with others in the holiness of who they are. It is God in communion with God—a oneness that manifests out of love.

CHAPTER 24

Forgiving Others

In society, we are raised to believe that our actions determine our worth. As children, when we behaved in ways that our parents, teachers, or other authority figures disapproved of, we were given a message that we did something wrong. But without explanation to help us understand the cause for others' reactions, we came to believe that *we* were wrong. When we feel guilt without rectification, it turns to shame, and our shame becomes a barrier that prevents us from knowing the truth of who we are. What we didn't realize as children is that the messages we received were not a reflection of our lovability but of the emotional and mental states of those who gave them. In woundedness, we wound; disconnected from the love within ourselves, we withhold love from others.

Throughout our lives, we have believed in the messages we received, yet have neglected to realize that we have *chosen* to believe them. In our Wounded Self, disconnected from God's love, we accepted others' interpretation of who we were. We are not victims of the world's judgment unless we give it the power to judge. When we take responsibility for our recovery and become a Loving Parent to our Inner Child, we are given the ability to correctly interpret the messages of others. We realize that we are worthy of unconditional love, so any message given to us that contradicts this truth is more easily recognized as false. The result is that we can practice forgiveness instead of retaliation. Knowing our own lovability, we are given the means to break the cycle of conditional love.

When we can practice forgiveness toward others, we show them that they are worthy of unconditional love—that they are not the false messages they were given, but a Child of God. This is how we transform the world, first by knowing our own lovability, and then by showing others' theirs. The practice of forgiveness, however, is a skill that we learn over time with our Inner Child and God. The impetus to retaliate or to love begins here. Perhaps one day, false messages will find no place in us to land, but our ability to deflect messages without passing them through to our Wounded Child is imperfect. We hear accusations, blame, attacks, and we feel them. Our recovery during these times is about how we respond to our hurt, not whether we feel hurt.

The process of forgiveness doesn't overlook or bypass our hurt. Before we can forgive, we must first turn toward our Wounded Child and connect with them in their feelings of rejection, betrayal, abandonment, anger, or grief. We hold them in their experience and acknowledge their pain, and doing so may open the door to our trauma. Often our present is tied to our past, and so our present hurt allows us to heal our past trauma. In connection with our Wounded Child, we rectify the false belief that we somehow deserved such treatment, whether then or now, and we transform our hurt and anger into a love that allows for forgiveness. When we are no longer in a place of hurt, there is no longer someone to blame. We can then share with others the truth of who they are regardless of their actions or the messages they may have given us.

Our practice of forgiveness doesn't condone mistreatment or abuse from others; it only demonstrates that we have learned how to respond to it in a way that breaks the cycle of conditional love. When our Wounded Child feels heard and seen, we can respond to others from our Loving Parent instead of from our Wounded Self and can communicate our hurt in a way that doesn't shame. Additionally, we communicate our needs and boundaries so that others may know when they have been unmet or crossed. This can help facilitate greater intimacy and awareness, which leads to more satisfying relationships. If others are unable or unwilling to honor our needs and boundaries, we can choose how or whether to remain in such relationships. Our connection to our Inner Child and God helps us to not be dependent upon others so that we can more easily let go of unhealthy relationships, even if doing so is painful.

THE MIRACLE OF FORGIVENESS

As we learn to practice forgiveness, we'll find that it doesn't always occur as quickly or as easily as we may like. This points not to the efficacy of forgiveness but to our intention in practicing it. For instance, if we pray for help in being free of resentment, we'll experience little relief unless we're also willing to feel the hurt of our Wounded Child. It is not likely God's will for us to simply say, "take this resentment from me," without engaging in the process that would allow for forgiveness to manifest. What would we get other than the relief of discomfort? We would not experience the intimacy that comes from being with our Inner Child or the awakening that results when we behold another once clouded by resentment, now enthroned with love.

> *And as we see the sinlessness in him come shining through the veil of guilt that shrouds the Son of God, we will behold in him the face of Christ, and understand that it is but our own.*[89]
>
> —IN A COURSE IN MIRACLES

The miracle of forgiveness not only shows others who they truly are but also reminds us of who we are. To help others know their inherent worth and lovability means that we have been brought to a place from which we can actually convey it. Forgiveness makes palpable the reality that we are not separate from the love we give, but a part of it. When we are grounded in God's love, we no longer interpret the actions or words of others from our Wounded Self; our communication to our Inner Child is that we are a Child of God, regardless of the world's judgment. When the truth within us is clear, illusion can find no foothold. We allow God's love to interpret our reality for us, and though we may experience the content and energy of another person's judgment, we recognize it is but woundedness that motivates them. As a result, we are able to take their behavior less personally and respond to them from truth and love.

The healing power that Jesus demonstrated in his life was that he saw others for who they were, beneath the various manifestations of their Wounded Self. His conviction of people's sinlessness, regardless of their awareness of it, is what gave sight to a blind man's eyes and gave life to those who were devoid of it. In Jesus's vision, they saw their own wholeness and were healed. The idea that Jesus "died for our sins" is a misinterpretation of his crucifixion. He was not made to be a scapegoat; his gift was in his message of forgiveness, which looked beyond the injuries others caused him to convey their inherent worth and lovability. There is no more powerful demonstration of this than when dying on the cross, Jesus said, "Father, forgive them, for they know not what they do."[90] The teaching here is not about God's forgiveness, but Jesus's. If Jesus were asking God to forgive those who harmed him, it paints a picture of God being judgmental and conditionally loving. However, the God that Jesus speaks of in the Gospels and the God we come to know within our own hearts is not so. God, being the source of unconditional love, can only give unconditional love. No judgment comes from unconditional love, and therefore no need for forgiveness.

If we can see Jesus as an archetype for our own potential, then it may be interpreted that he, in that moment of supplication, was actually speaking from his Core Child to his Loving Parent, whom his Child referred to as "Father." Jesus was human and felt injury as a human. No matter how much healing we have undergone, whenever we experience harm from another, it hurts, and if severe enough, may provoke the reaction of our Wounded Self. For Jesus, such reaction was not in any response made to those who harmed him but in whatever resistance he may have felt toward practicing forgiveness. When our Wounded Self is activated, we share their consciousness, and as a result, are in a state of mind that is less able to love and forgive unconditionally. It may be that at that moment, Jesus's Core Child—who was connected to the truth—sensed Jesus's own resistance and therefore asked his "Father" to "forgive them." The significance of this teaching is that Jesus *did* forgive them. His ascension was evidence of that. When we can practice forgiveness toward those who harm us, realizing "they know not what they do," we too make possible our own ascension, not out of body, but into higher consciousness.

CHAPTER 25

Sharing Ourselves with Others

In relationships, we can share ourselves with others—our whole selves. Though we may not have been taught this was possible or even an option growing up, today it is. The hard work and transformation we have undergone throughout this process of recovery has shown us how freeing it is to embody and express all of who we are. However, taking this step with others can feel scary if we were given messages that it's *not* okay to be who we are, share how we're feeling, or to reach out for help and support. We may have touched these wounds and fears already, but they will come up again and again until we experience the opposite of what we learned.

Our relationships become a place where we can heal together. We share the full spectrum of our humanity and our divinity: our sadness, grief, depression, anger, anxiety, playfulness, excitement, joy, and love. It is a process. We all begin where we are and quickly discover our edges. Simply stating how we're feeling may be our edge, especially if it is an emotion we were taught to keep hidden. For instance, our Wounded Self may fear that if we share our sadness, we won't be met with compassion or understanding, but rejection. If that was our experience when we were young, our Wounded Self believes it will happen again, and will reinforce the message that sharing how we feel is not okay. They may, therefore, believe it's safer to not even take the risk than put our vulnerability on the line. However, if we desire to have intimate relationships, we have to take these risks. When we are in the practice of being a Loving Parent to our Inner Child and in connection with God, we can choose to share ourselves, knowing we have the tools to respond to whatever happens.

HEALING IN RELATIONSHIPS

In relationships, we learn to share our experiences without making others responsible for it. We no longer blame others for how we're feeling or look to them to change how we're feeling. Yet being a Loving Parent to our Inner Child does not mean we have to heal alone. We need each other on this journey. Sometimes we can be so adamant in our desire to change old behaviors that we unknowingly swing the pendulum of our Wounded Self strategies to the other side. Instead of codependency, we practice obstinate self-sufficiency or vice versa. Being in relationships with others is not so much finding the balance between the two but an entirely new dynamic.

It takes a tremendous amount of courage to step over the line of our conditioning and remain open to what occurs. Each new risk brings its own fears, but when we take them with someone who shares our values, we create a relationship that supports our vision. We excavate new territory together, and the steps we each take benefit the other. For instance, when we choose to share how we're feeling with our partner, we open the door to intimacy and vulnerability, which gives them permission to share with us as well. Over time the freedom we experience in relationship with our Inner Child and God is the culture we create in relationships with others. Instead of the inhibiting messages of our past, we offer the liberating messages of a new paradigm: *"It's okay to be as you are,"* *"It's safe to share your feelings,"* and *"You're loved and supported in your experience, whatever it is."* Hearing and feeling these messages fortifies the foundation of our recovery.

When we create safety in relationships with others, we feel more permission to be all of who we are. Gradually a new consciousness forms. The healing of society, of the entire universe, is an act of unconditional love; it begins in relationship with ourselves and extends outward into our relationships with others. Instead of passing on intergenerational trauma, we pass on intergenerational health.

If we want to evolve as a society, if we want the collective consciousness of the human race to shift, we *must* create new norms that support the full, uninhibited expression of who we are. When we do this, we return to the Garden of Eden, naked and without shame. God becomes a living reality that we experience together, and the world becomes a place of light.

CHAPTER 26

Remembering Who We Are

This process of recovery can be its own reward and not a means to an end. We may not know where God is leading us, but we come to trust that what is happening in our lives is a part of the journey. God's will for us is to love ourselves and others unconditionally. All of our circumstances, relationships, and challenges are given to us for this purpose. When we look for God's gifts through the eyes of our human condition—from our Wounded Self—we may not see them. We may lose hope and think that all of our work has been for nothing. But if we hold faith and remain open to God's guidance, we will know that our experience is for our growth and is our blessing.

On a fundamental level, God cares for us regardless of whether we care for ourselves, but it is when we choose to care for ourselves that we manifest the love, peace, and joy that God wills for us to experience. We learn that what is most loving is being *here* in our experience right *now*. This is where our Inner Child needs us; this is how we heal. It is this being *with*, this choosing to embody and be present to all of what *is* that is the real demonstration of our willingness to recover. God asks us to trust this moment—that where we are and how we are is perfectly okay. God asks us to love this moment and to let this act of loving be an end in itself.

The path of recovery is our exodus from Egypt; it is living the teachings of Jesus; it is rewriting everything we have learned and believed. Going against the grain of our conditioning is a lot of work. We learn that we have a choice in how we live and that we are responsible for making this choice. Yet over time, after dozens, hundreds, and thousands of choices to act differently, acting differently becomes acting naturally. Choosing what is most loving becomes second nature, and it is the river that takes us home.

Notes

1 Margaret Paul and Erika Chopich, Inner Bonding® Educational Technologies, Inc. (2020).
2 *A Course in Miracles* (Mill Valley: Foundation for Inner Peace, 2007).
3 Neale Donald Walsch, *The Complete Conversations with God: An Uncommon Dialogue* (Charlottesville: Hampton Roads Publishing Company, Inc., 2005).
4 "Preface" in *A Course in Miracles*, vii.
5 Mary D. Salter Ainsworth et al., *Patterns of Attachment: A Psychological Study of the Strange Situation* (New York: Psychology Press, 2015).
6 Margaret Paul, *Do I Have to Give Up Me to Be Loved by God?* (Deerfield Beach: Health Communications Inc., 1999).
7 Jeremiah Abrams, *Reclaiming the Inner Child* (Los Angeles: Jeremy P. Tarcher, Inc., 1990), 1.
8 *A Course in Miracles.*
9 Paul, *Do I Have to Give Up Me to Be Loved by God?*

10 Gen. 2:17 Tanakh.

11 Gen. 3:5 KJV.

12 Gen. 3:9 NIV.

13 *Ibid.*, 3:10.

14 *Ibid.*, 3:11.

15 Gen. 1:31 Tanakh.

16 *Ibid.*, 1:28.

17 Walsch, *Conversations with God.*

18 Paul, *Do I Have to Give Up Me to Be Loved by God?*, 119.

19 *Ibid.*

20 Paul, *Do I Have to Give Up Me to Be Loved by God?*

21 Carl G. Jung, *The Collected Works of C.G. Jung*, Vol. 8: *Structure and Dynamics of the Psyche*, ed. Gerhard Adler and R.F.C. Hull (Princeton: Princeton University Press, 1969), para 270.

22 Ainsworth et al., *Patterns of Attachment.*

23 Mary Main and Judith Solomon, "Discovery of an Insecure-Disorganized/Disoriented Attachment Pattern," in *Affective Development in Infancy*, ed. Thomas B. Brazelton and Michael Yogman (Norwood: Ablex, 1986), 95–124.

24 Ainsworth et al., *Patterns of Attachment.*

25 Mary D. Salter Ainsworth, "Attachment as Related to Mother-Infant Interaction," in *Advances in the Study of Behavior* Vol. 9, ed. Jay S. Rosenblatt, Robert A. Hinde, Colin Beer, and Marie-Claire Busnel (New York: Academic Press, Inc., 1979), 1-51.

26 Main and Solomon, "Discovery of an Insecure-Disorganized/Disoriented Attachment Pattern."

27 *Ibid.*

28 Ainsworth et al., *Patterns of Attachment.*

29 *Ibid.*

30 *Ibid.*

31 Ainsworth, "Mother-Infant Interaction."

32 Marinus H. van IJzendoorn and Pieter M. Kroonenberg, "Cross-Cultural Patterns of Attachment: A Meta-Analysis of the Strange Situation Procedure," *Child Development* 59, no. 1 (1988): 147-156.

33 M. Ann Easterbrooks and Michael E. Lamb, "The Relationship Between Quality of Infant-Mother Attachment and Infant Competence in Initial Encounter with Peers," *Child Development* 50, no. 2 (1979): 380-387.

34 van IJzendoorn and Kroonenberg, "Cross-Cultural Patterns," 153.

35 Byron Egeland and Ellen A. Farber, "Infant-Mother Attachment: Factors Related to Its Development and Changes over Time," *Child Development* 55, no. 3 (1984): 753–771; Janice H. Kennedy and Roger Bakeman, "The Early Mother-Infant Relationship and Social Competence with Peers and Adults at Three Years," *Journal of Psychology* 116, no. 1 (1984): 23-34; Karen Schneider-Rosen and Dante Cicchetti, "The Relationship between Affect and Cognition in Maltreated Infants: Quality of Attachment and the Development of Visual Self-Recognition," *Child Development* 55, no. 2 (1984): 648–658.

36 van IJzendoorn and Kroonenberg, "Cross-Cultural Patterns," 153–154.

37 Ainsworth et al., *Patterns of Attachment.*

38 Ainsworth et al., *Patterns of Attachment.*

39 Main and Solomon, "Discovery of an Insecure-Disorganized/Disoriented Attachment Pattern," 112.

40 Allan N. Schore, "Dysregulation of the Right Brain: A Fundamental Mechanism of Traumatic Attachment and the Psychopathogensis of Posttraumatic Stress Disorder," *Australian and New Zealand Journal of Psychiatry* 36, no. 1 (2002): 9–30.

41 Daniel Hill, *Affect Regulation Theory: A Clinical Model* (New York: W.W. Norton & Company, 2015).

42 Allan N. Schore, "The Effects of Early Relational Trauma on Right Brain Development, Affect Regulation, and Infant Mental Health," *Infant Mental Health Journal* 22, no. 1-2 (2001): 201–269.

43 Schore, "Dysregulation of Right Brain."

44 Schore, "Early Relational Trauma," 210.

45 *Ibid.*

46 Ainsworth et al., *Patterns of Attachment.*

47 *Ibid.*

48 Schore, "Early Relational Trauma," 211.

49 Mary Main and Judith Solomon, "Procedures for Identifying Infants as Disorganized/Disoriented during the Ainsworth Strange Situation," In *Attachment in the Preschool Years: Theory, Research, and Intervention*, ed. Mark T. Greenberg, Dante Cicchetti, and E. Mark Cummings (Chicago: The University of Chicago Press, 1990), 132.

50 Vicki Carlson et al., "Disorganized/Disoriented Attachment

Relationships in Maltreated Infants," *Developmental Psychology* 25, no. 4 (1989): 525-531.

51 Mary Main and Erik Hesse, "Parents' Unresolved Traumatic Experiences Are Related to Infant Disorganized Attachment Status: Is Frightened and/or Frightening Parental Behavior the Linking Mechanism?," In *Attachment in the Preschool Years: Theory, Research, and Intervention*, ed. Mark T. Greenberg, Dante Cicchetti, and E. Mark Cummings (Chicago: The University of Chicago Press, 1990), 163.

52 Schore, "Early Relational Trauma," 234.

53 Hill, *Affect Regulation Theory*.

54 Rabindranath Tagore, *Gitanjali* (New York: Scribner Poetry, 1997), 45.

55 *A Course in Miracles*, T-29.IV.4:1.

56 Gabor Maté, *In the Realm of Hungry Ghosts: Close Encounters with Addiction* (Berkeley: North Atlantic Books, 2010), 236.

57 American Psychiatric Association, *Diagnostic and Statistical Manual of Mental Disorders*, Fifth Edition (Arlington, VA: American Psychiatric Association, 2013).

58 David H. Gleaves, "The Sociocognitive Model of Dissociative Identity Disorder: A Reexamination of the Evidence," *Psychological Bulletin* 120, no. 1 (1996): 42–59.

59 Martin Buber, *The Legend of The Baal-Shem* (New York: Schocken Books, Inc., 1969), 25.

60 *ACA Fellowship Text* (Torrence, CA: Adult Children of Alcoholics ®/Dysfunctional Families World Service Organization, Inc., 2006).

61 Tanakh.

62 Exod. 14:30 Tanakh.

63 Luke 1:37 KJV.

64 Luke 1:38 ESV.

65 Matt. 3:16 ESV.

66 Gen. 1:27 NIV.

67 Ainsworth et al., *Patterns of Attachment*.

68 Gen. Tanakh.

69 Rom. 7:15–19 NIV.

70 Rom. 7:18 NIV.

71 Matt. 12:25 KJV.

72 Luke 15:13-14 KJV.

73 Luke 15: 17-18 KJV.

74 *A Course in Miracles*, T-11.VI.7:1.

75 Ainsworth et al., *Patterns of Attachment*.

76 Marvin Meyer, *The Gospel of Thomas: The Hidden Sayings of Jesus* (New York: HarperSanFrancisco, 1992), 37.

77 Gen. 3:6-9 KJV.

78 Meyer, *The Gospel of Thomas*, 37.

79 *A Course in Miracles*, W-p1.153.6:1–2.

80 Kahlil Gibran, *Jesus the Son of Man: His Words and His Deeds as Told and Recorded by Those Who Knew Him* (New York: Knopf, 1995), 17.

81 Walsch, *Conversations with God*.

82 Luke 15:31–32 NIV.

83 Gen. 3:4–5 Tanakh.

84 *A Course in Miracles*, M-5.I.1:1–2.

85 Matt. 18:3 NIV.

86 John 1:51 ESV.

87 *A Course in Miracles*, T-6.I.13:2.

88 Matt. 19:29 NIV.

89 *A Course in Miracles*, P-2.V.7:8.

90 Luke 23:34 ESV.

Bibliography

ACA Fellowship Text. Torrence: Adult Children of Alcoholics ®/ Dysfunctional Families World Service Organization, Inc., 2006.

A Course in Miracles. Mill Valley: Foundation for Inner Peace, 2007.

Abrams, Jeremiah. *Reclaiming the Inner Child*. Los Angeles: Jeremy P. Tarcher, Inc., 1990.

Ainsworth, Mary D. Salter. "Attachment as Related to Mother-Infant Interaction." *Advances in the Study of Behavior* Vol. 9, edited by Jay. S. Rosenblatt, Robert A. Hinde, Colin Beer, and Marie-Claire Busnel, 1–51. New York: Academic Press, Inc., 1979.

Ainsworth, Mary D. Salter, Mary C. Blehar, Everett Waters, and Sally N. Wall. *Patterns of Attachment: A Psychological Study of the Strange Situation*. New York: Psychology Press, 2015.

American Psychiatric Association. *Diagnostic and Statistical Manual of Mental Disorders*, Fifth Edition. Arlington, VA: American Psychiatric Association, 2013.

Buber, Martin. *The Legend of The Baal-Shem*. New York: Schocken Books Inc., 1969.

Carlson, Vicki, Dante Cicchetti, Douglas Barnett, and Karen Braunwald. "Disorganized/Disoriented Attachment Relationships in Maltreated Infants." *Developmental Psychology* 25, no. 4 (1989): 525–531.

Easterbrooks, M. Ann, and Michael E. Lamb. "The Relationship between Quality of Infant-Mother Attachment and Infant Competence in Initial Encounter with Peers." *Child Development* 50, no. 2 (1979): 380–387.

Egeland, Byron, and Ellen A. Farber. "Infant-Mother Attachment. Factors Related to Its Development and Changes over Time." *Child Development* 55, no. 3 (1984): 753–771.

Gibran, Kahlil. *Jesus the Son of Man: His Words and His Deeds as Told and Recorded by Those Who Knew Him*. New York: Knopf, 1995.

Gleaves, David H. "The Sociocognitive Model of Dissociative Identity Disorder: A Reexamination of the Evidence." *Psychological Bulletin* 120, no. 1 (1996): 42–59.

Hill, Daniel. *Affect Regulation Theory: A Clinical Model*. New York: W.W. Norton & Company, 2015.

Jung, Carl G. *The Collected Works of C.G. Jung* Vol. 8, *Structure and Dynamics of the Psyche*, edited by Gerhard Adler and R.F.C. Hull. Princeton: Princeton University Press, 1969.

Kennedy, Janice H., and Roger Bakeman. "The Early Mother-Infant Relationship and Social Competence with Peers and Adults at Three Years." *Journal of Psychology* 116, no. 1

(1984): 23–34.

Main, Mary, and Erik Hesse. "Parents' Unresolved Traumatic Experiences Are Related to Infant Disorganized Attachment Status: Is Frightened and/or Frightening Parental Behavior the Linking Mechanism?" In *Attachment in the Preschool Years: Theory, Research, and Intervention*, edited by Mark T. Greenberg, Dante Cicchetti, and E. Mark Cummings, 161–182. Chicago: The University of Chicago Press, 1990.

Main, Mary, and Judith Solomon. "Procedures for Identifying Infants as Disorganized/Disoriented during the Ainsworth Strange Situation." In *Attachment in the Preschool Years: Theory, Research, and Intervention*, edited by Mark T. Greenberg, Dante Cicchetti, and E. Mark Cummings, 121-160. Chicago: The University of Chicago Press, 1990.

Main, Mary, and Judith Solomon. "Discovery of an Insecure-Disorganized/Disoriented Attachment Pattern." In *Affective Development in Infancy,* edited by Thomas B. Brazelton and Michael Yogman, 95–124. Norwood: Ablex, 1986.

Maté, Gabor. *In the Realm of Hungry Ghosts: Close Encounters with Addiction.* Berkeley: North Atlantic Books, 2010.

Meyer, Marvin. *The Gospel of Thomas: The Hidden Sayings Of Jesus.* New York: HarperSanFrancisco, 1992.

Paul, Margaret. *Do I Have to Give Up Me to Be Loved by God?* Deerfield Beach: Health Communications, Inc., 1999.

Paul, Margaret, and Erika Chopich. Inner Bonding® Educational Technologies, Inc., 2020.

Schneider-Rosen, Karen, and Dante Cicchetti. "The Relationship between Affect and Cognition in Maltreated Infants: Quality of Attachment and the Development of Visual Self-Recognition." *Child Development* 55, no. 2 (1984): 648–658.

Schore, Allan N. "The Effects of Early Relational Trauma on Right Brain Development, Affect Regulation, and Infant Mental Health." *Infant Mental Health Journal* 22, no. 1–2 (2001): 201–269.

Schore, Allan N. "Dysregulation of the Right Brain: A Fundamental Mechanism of Traumatic Attachment and the Psychopathogenesis of Posttraumatic Stress Disorder," *Australian & New Zealand Journal of Psychiatry* 36, no. 1 (2002): 9–30.

Tagore, Rabindranath. *Gitanjali.* New York: Scribner Poetry, 1997.

Tanakh: A New Translation of The Holy Scriptures According to the Traditional Hebrew Text: Torah, Nevi'im, Kethuvim. Philadelphia: Jewish Publication Society, 1985.

van IJzendoorn, Marinus H., and Pieter M. Kroonenberg. "Cross-Cultural Patterns of Attachment: A Meta-Analysis of the Strange Situation." *Child Development* 59, no. 1, (1988): 147–156.

Walsch, Neale Donald. *The Complete Conversations with God: An Uncommon Dialogue.* Charlottesville: Hampton Roads Publishing Company, Inc., 2005.

Copyrights and Permissions

- All quotes are from *A Course in Miracles*, copyright © 1992, 1999, 2007, by the Foundation for Inner Peace, 448 Ignacio Blvd., #306, Novato, CA 94949, www.acim.org and info@acim.org, used with permission.
- Scriptures taken from the Holy Bible, New International Version®, NIV®. Copyright © 1973, 1978, 1984, 2011 by Biblica, Inc.™ Used by permission of Zondervan. All rights reserved worldwide. www.zondervan.com The "NIV" and "New International Version" are trademarks registered in the United States Patent and Trademark Office by Biblica, Inc.™
- Scripture quotations are from the ESV® Bible (The Holy Bible, English Standard Version®), copyright © 2001 by Crossway, a publishing ministry of Good News Publishers. Used by permission. All rights reserved.

CPSIA information can be obtained
at www.ICGtesting.com
Printed in the USA
BVHW030229211220
596152BV00014B/133